MAKING PRO BONO A PRIORITY:

A BAR LEADER'S HANDBOOK

ABA Center for Pro Bono
A Project of the Consortium on Legal Services and the Public

Standing Committee on Lawyers' Public Service Responsibility

Section of Litigation

AMERICAN BAR ASSOCIATION
541 N. Fairbanks Court
Chicago, Illinois 60611

SECOND EDITION

This manual has not been reviewed by the House of Delegates or the Board of Governors of the American Bar Association and, accordingly, should not be construed as representing policy of the American Bar Association.

American Bar Association
541 N. Fairbanks Court
Chicago, Illinois 60611

Consortium on Legal Services and the Public, Esther F. Lardent, Chair

Standing Committee on Lawyers' Public Service Responsibility
James L. Baillie, Chair

Steering Committee, Center for Pro Bono, Robert E. Hirshon, Chair

Section of Litigation
Lawrence J. Fox, Chair

Second Edition

July 1996

ISBN 1-57073-346-5
1.8K

MAKING PRO BONO A PRIORITY:
A BAR LEADER'S HANDBOOK

TABLE OF CONTENTS

MAKING PRO BONO A PRIORITY: A BAR LEADER'S HANDBOOK

FOREWORD

At its August 1995 meeting, the ABA House of Delegates adopted a resolution that urges the ABA, along with other bar associations, to make the expansion of pro bono legal services by practicing lawyers a critical priority. The resolution, which was co-sponsored by the ABA's Standing Committee on Lawyers' Public Service Responsibility (SCLPSR), Section of Litigation, Consortium on Legal Services and the Public, and a number of other ABA and non-ABA entities, also urges bar associations to develop effective and innovative strategies for promoting pro bono activities.

The resolution encourages bar associations to work in cooperation with existing pro bono and legal services programs in developing their strategies and to devote sufficient resources to ensure that such strategies can be properly implemented. In addition, the resolution provides examples of several activities that bars should consider in formulating their pro bono efforts.

The Center for Pro Bono, SCLPSR, and the Section of Litigation have developed this handbook as a tool for bar leaders to use in implementing the ABA House of Delegates' resolution. These entities are ready to provide whatever help is necessary in assisting bar leaders with the development of new and innovative pro bono projects and policies. Included in this handbook are:

* the description of an extensive range of strategies bar associations should consider as part of their pro bono commitment;

* examples of how particular strategies have been applied by selected bar associations around the country;

* samples of selected materials reflecting the manner in which a particular strategy has been implemented by a bar association;

* contact names and phone numbers to assist bar leaders in gathering additional information and materials;

* a list of additional resources which bar leaders can utilize in the development of pro bono activities within their association.

The ABA has worked with many groups and individuals -- including dozens of bar associations -- to defeat the imposition of increased restrictions on and decreased funding for Legal Services Corporation-funded programs. These efforts have not been completely successful. Accordingly, there have been significant changes in the structure, operation and staffing of legal services programs. As these changes continue to unfold in the months and years ahead, the need for bar associations to commit to the development of organized, coordinated and institutionalized pro bono efforts will become increasingly important.

The changes that are taking place in the legal services delivery system provide significant opportunities for the ABA, state, local, minority and specialty bars, legal services and pro bono programs, individual lawyers and others to develop a new vision of serving the legal needs of persons of limited means. ***Making Pro Bono a Priority: A Bar Leader's Handbook*** has been developed to provide bar leaders with the guidance and resources they need to take full advantage of these opportunities.

Funds for the initial publication and distribution of this handbook were provided by the ABA's Section of Litigation. Principal credit for its drafting goes to Bonnie Allen, Assistant Staff Counsel for the Center for Pro Bono. Editorial assistance was provided by SCLPSR's Pro Bono Policy Subcommittee (Justin Vigdor, Dean David Hall, Curtis Caton and Jim Baillie); Victor Geminiani, Co-Chair, Section of Litigation Pro Bono and Public Interest Practice Committee; Ann Barker, Coordinator of the Litigation Assistance Partnership Project, a project of the Section of Litigation; and Beverly Groudine, SCLPSR Assistant Committee Counsel.

As a bar leader you have the opportunity to provide direction and leadership for the organization and the members you represent. There can be no greater calling than to use this opportunity to lead your bar and its members on a continuing crusade for equal access to justice. This ***Bar Leader's Handbook*** is a road map to help you on this important journey. Thank you for your commitment to pro bono.

Esther F. Lardent	Chair, Consortium on Legal Services and the Public
Robert E. Hirshon	Chair, Steering Committee for the Center for Pro Bono
James L. Baillie	Chair, Standing Committee on Lawyers' Public Service Responsibility
Lawrence J. Fox	Chair, Section of Litigation

INTRODUCTION

Recent studies indicate that the legal needs of only an average of twenty percent of low and moderate income persons in this country are met. In view of the growth of poverty, and the reduction of funding and increased restrictions regarding federally-funded legal services organizations, the need for pro bono legal services is greater than ever. For purposes of this handbook, ***"pro bono legal services"*** **are free civil legal services rendered by attorneys not employed by legal services programs to persons who cannot afford counsel.**

Bar leaders are encouraged to work with the judiciary, legal services organizations, funders, law firms, other social services providers and client groups in their communities to design integrated strategies for addressing these unmet legal needs. Access to justice is dependent upon the availability of legal help. Because of their stature, organizational structure and resources, bar associations are uniquely situated to spearhead the effort to promote and coordinate the pro bono component of an integrated strategy. Bar leaders, in particular, are in a position to influence and direct the expansion of legal services to the poor. In addition to influencing the structure of the bar to promote pro bono activities, bar leaders and candidates for bar leadership positions should demonstrate their support for pro bono and legal services through pro bono service, and service on boards that provide legal services to persons of limited means.

This handbook will discuss four models through which bar associations can play an integral role in the delivery of legal services to persons of limited means:

> **Allocation of resources to promote pro bono activities**
>
> **Adoption of rules and policies that promote pro bono participation**
>
> **Support of existing pro bono programs and activities through recruiting, fundraising, training, recognition and publicity**
>
> **Creation and administration of bar-sponsored pro bono projects and programs, including state support programs and direct delivery systems**

Specific ways in which bar associations around the country have applied these models are discussed in this handbook. The attachments included at the end of each of the four sections of the handbook represent examples of the specific application of these models. For more information, bar leaders are encouraged to communicate with the referenced contact persons. In addition, bar leaders should consult the *Standards For Programs Providing Civil Pro Bono Legal Services To Persons Of Limited Means.*

Bar leaders also should access the resources of the ABA Center for Pro Bono, which serves as a national pro bono support center. Among the resources available through the Center are: the annual Pro Bono Conference (co-sponsored with the ABA Standing Committee on Lawyers' Public Service Responsibility); Info Packs on a variety of pro bono-related issues, including recruiting, training, clinics, and strategic planning; the Peer Consulting Project, which provides on-site technical assistance to pro bono programs and bar associations; and the Pro Bono Hotline, which provides immediate information on pro bono topics.

Information requests should be directed to:

The ABA Center for Pro Bono Hotline: (312) 988-5769

OR

The ABA Center for Pro Bono Staff:
541 N. Fairbanks Court
Chicago, IL 60611

Steven Scudder, Staff Counsel
(312) 988-5768

Bonnie Allen, Assistant Staff Counsel
(312) 988-5773

Bridget Howard, Administrator
(312) 988-5789

BEFORE YOU GET STARTED...

Bar leaders should consider some basic issues before undertaking a major pro bono initiative.

Self-Assessment

Before launching a major pro bono initiative, bar leaders should assess the current status of the pro bono effort in their legal community. This "pro bono checkup" evaluates various factors affecting the level of pro bono participation in the bar, including the extent and scope of existing organized pro bono activity, level of financial support for existing programs, and mechanisms already in place within the bar association that promote pro bono activity (e.g. resolutions promoting pro bono, pro bono committees, and awards ceremonies that recognize outstanding pro bono efforts by attorneys).

Another aspect of self-assessment involves an analysis of both the unmet legal needs of persons of limited means, and the legal resources that are available to meet those needs. Bar leaders should work with local legal services providers, the judiciary, social services providers, and client groups to determine the greatest areas of unmet legal needs. The very process of initiating a dialogue and discussing the extent of the need and how it should be addressed is likely to generate support for pro bono programs. This assessment and dialogue will lay the groundwork for priority-setting and recruiting volunteer attorneys to render legal services where they are needed most. While pro bono services should be based on client need, they must be balanced against the expertise and willingness of the private bar to handle certain types of legal matters.

Finally, bar associations must identity and address the obstacles to the development of an effective pro bono delivery system. Obstacles may include antagonistic attitudes toward organized pro bono activity, as well as logistical challenges, such as geographic distances between clients and attorneys. Rural areas present particular obstacles to the development of pro bono delivery systems. Loosely organized bar associations in rural areas often meet infrequently, limiting opportunities for bar leaders to recruit pro bono attorneys. In addition, geographic distances may hinder the ability and willingness of attorneys to render pro bono services to clients in rural areas.

Minimizing Opposition to Maximize Opportunity

An important step in building support for pro bono in the bar is minimizing opposition. Bar leaders must assess the extent to which groups and individuals oppose organized pro bono legal services. Some attorneys erroneously fear that organized pro bono activity is likely to lead to mandatory pro bono service; others believe that it is unnecessary to institutionalize pro bono because attorneys already are doing it in their own practices. Bar leaders should solicit input from attorneys and address their interests and concerns. Pro bono initiatives will be more successful if they have widespread attorney support.

Building Support for Pro Bono in the Bar

Once bar leaders have engaged in self-assessment and addressed opposition, they must build support for pro bono in the bar. Education is the first step. Bar leaders must inform bar members of the overwhelming need for legal services to persons of limited means. The results of national, statewide and local legal needs studies should be made available to the bar. Many attorneys are unaware of the inadequacies of the current delivery system in meeting the needs of persons of limited means. Judges can be very helpful. As courtrooms become increasingly flooded with unrepresented litigants, judges are highly motivated to call upon the private bar to assist in finding solutions to the problem of unequal access to legal representation.

Building a base of support for pro bono begins by identifying where support already exists. In many states and local communities, the bar foundation, federally-funded legal services organizations, and other not-for-profit legal services providers already are engaged in the delivery of legal services to persons of limited means. Each of these groups should be brought into the bar association's planning initiative as early as possible. A coordinated approach helps to avoid unnecessary duplication of efforts and competition for volunteers and funding.

Further, the bar association should include a cross-section of the legal community in its efforts to develop support for pro bono activities. In addition to the groups listed above, judges, bar leaders from major practice sections and minority and specialty bar associations, representatives from large and small law firms, solo practitioners, directors of legal services programs, representatives of social services organizations that serve persons of limited means, and representatives of client groups should be included in the planning effort.

Commitment of the Bar

Finally, the bar association must make a commitment to enhance pro bono activities, and it must be willing to make that commitment part of the overall structure of the bar. This commitment should be reflected in pro bono service by bar leadership, the structuring of bar committees, staffing decisions, and long-range planning.

SECTION 1

SECTION 1: ALLOCATION OF RESOURCES TO PROMOTE PRO BONO ACTIVITIES

Creation of Bar Committees

<u>Discussion</u>

One important method of promoting pro bono within a bar association is through the committee structure. Committees are an effective tool for educating bar members about the need for pro bono services, accomplishing tasks, and conducting long-term planning and administration. Many bar associations create committees that focus on issues related to availability of legal services and equal access to the legal system for persons of limited means. In some cases, pro bono service is considered by these committees or subcommittees as one piece of an integrated strategy for overcoming access to justice problems. In others, separate committees are created to focus exclusively on pro bono activity. In either situation, the committee should reflect a cross-section of the bar, including but not limited to representatives from major practice sections, the judiciary, law firms, legal services organizations, government lawyers, corporate counsel attorneys, minority bars, and young lawyers.

Bar associations should include pro bono committees as part of their standing committee structure. The bar president or president-elect should sit on these committees, at least in an ex-officio capacity. Special committees may be appropriate for limited and specific purposes, such as legal needs studies, program assessment, fundraising, or implementation of mandatory reporting or service. A standing committee is needed, however, to provide the overall planning, organization and administration of pro bono activities. In many states, there is a statewide standing pro bono committee that works in conjunction with local bar committees in various counties or judicial districts. It is important that bar associations adequately support standing pro bono committees with staff resources, and that staff performing oversight functions of various pro bono committees work together to maximize efficiency.

In addition to standing or special committees that report directly to the bar's board of directors, many practice sections also set up pro bono committees that focus on how lawyers in their section can provide pro bono services to clients with needs in the subject area of their practice. Minority or specialty bars may also form their own pro bono committees. It is important for section and specialty bar pro bono committees to coordinate with the standing committee of the bar association to avoid unnecessary duplication of efforts, to share information, and to strategize together when appropriate.

Pros

- ☞ The inclusion of pro bono committees in the bar structure demonstrates the bar's commitment to pro bono efforts as an integral part of its mission and long-range planning. It also provides the long-range planning necessary to implement pro bono activities over the long-term.
- ☞ Pro bono committees can serve as effective advisory boards to pro bono programs.
- ☞ Pro bono committees provide an excellent mechanism for generating interest in pro bono activities, educating bar members regarding the need for pro bono services, and offering members opportunities to assume specific responsibilities.
- ☞ Pro bono committees can stabilize and maintain pro bono activities through changes in the leadership and staff of the bar association.

Cons

- ☞ Resources are needed to staff or support committees.
- ☞ Without a clear role, committees may lose appropriate focus and divert time and energy away from addressing critical needs.

Contacts

Florida Voluntary Attorney Pro Bono Plan
Staff Contact: Kent Spuhler, Director, Florida Legal Services, Inc. (904) 385-7900
Volunteer Contact: Honorable William Van Nortwick, Jr., First District Court of Appeal (904) 488-6151

Washington State Bar Association Legal Aid Committee
Staff Contact: Joan Fairbanks, Director, Access to Justice Board (206) 727-8282
Volunteer Contact: Paul Stritmatter (360) 533-2710

New York State Bar Association
Staff Contact: Tony Cassino, Director, Department of Pro Bono Affairs (518) 487-5640
Volunteer Contact: Joseph Genova (212) 530-5532

Lafayette Parish Bar Association (Louisiana)
Staff Contact: Stasia Herbert (318) 237-4000
Volunteer Contact: Kay Karre (318) 237-2660

Toledo Bar Association (Ohio)
Staff Contact: Susan Martin, Executive Director (419) 242-7032 x 3001

Examples

Rule 4-6.5, Rules Regulating the Florida Bar
Florida Voluntary Attorney Plan (Attachment 1-A)

Washington State Bar Association Legal Aid Committee Volunteer Attorney Legal Services Action Plan (Attachment 1-B)

Commitment of Staff Resources

Discussion

The coordination and promotion of pro bono activities by bar associations can be time-consuming and administratively intensive. Volunteers can participate in pro bono committees and take on discrete assignments relating to planning, recruiting, training, publicity and fundraising. It generally is not feasible, however, for volunteers to be solely responsible for the day-to-day operation of a pro bono program or overall coordination of the bar's pro bono efforts. As a result, many bar associations hire a staff person or persons to perform these functions, or contribute to another organization that provides that support.

Staff support takes many forms. Some state bar associations employ staff to manage a statewide pro bono delivery program. The staff may be responsible for supervising client intake and case referral, recruiting and training pro bono attorneys, organizing recognition events, handling public relations, fundraising, and working with local pro bono programs throughout the state on matters related to direct delivery of pro bono legal services. In other states, where there is no statewide direct delivery, the bar association employs a state support director to coordinate statewide pro bono planning and staff standing committees, as well as to support local pro bono programs. Finally, some state support directors perform both a direct delivery and support function. In any case, the statewide pro bono coordinator should work closely with bar leaders, members of the judiciary, funders, and legal services project directors to plan statewide strategies for the enhancement of pro bono activities. A state support program or statewide direct delivery program is in place in the majority of states.

Similarly, some local bar associations employ staff to manage a bar-sponsored pro bono direct delivery program, or to coordinate with or support other pro bono programs in the community.

While not all bar associations are in a position to commit a full-time staff person to coordinate pro bono activities, bar associations are encouraged to allocate at least a portion of the staff's time to pro bono matters.

The role of staff is discussed more fully in Section 4 of this handbook.

Pros

- ☞ The allocation of staff resources to pro bono matters demonstrates a visible commitment by the bar to institutionalize pro bono activities as an integral part of the bar's mission.
- ☞ Paid staff relieve volunteers of day-to-day administrative responsibilities, thus freeing up volunteers to concentrate on policy, long-range planning and specific assignments relating to increasing pro bono participation among bar members.
- ☞ The coordination of pro bono matters by staff helps to maintain consistency amidst changing bar leadership.

Cons

- ☞ Paid staff requires the expenditure of financial resources.
- ☞ Some bar members may perceive the hiring of staff as the creation of unnecessary bureaucracy.

Contacts

State Bar of California, Office of Legal Services
Staff Contacts: Eve Hershcopf (415) 561-8213 and Sharon Ngim (415) 561-8267, Pro Bono Program Developers
Volunteer Contact: Jack Londen (415) 677-7415

South Carolina Bar Pro Bono Program
Staff Contact: Donna Stobbe, Executive Director (803) 799-6653
Volunteer Contact: George Cauthen (803) 733-9404

Public Counsel (Los Angeles, California)
Staff Contact: Steven Nissen, Executive Director (213) 385-2977 x 104
Volunteer Contact: Robert Williams (213) 620-1780

Legal Aid Society of the Orange County Bar Association (Florida)
Staff Contact: Catherine Tucker, Executive Director (407) 841-8310
Volunteer Contact: Lawrence Matthews (407) 872-2200

Coordination of Integrated Pro Bono Planning and Action Plans

Discussion

Because of their stature, organizational structure and resources, bars often take the lead in coordinating pro bono efforts within the legal community. However, they should not act alone. Judges, funders, representatives of law firms, legal services organizations, social services providers and client groups should be included in the dialogue and planning process as early as possible.

In addition, pro bono activity should not be viewed in a vacuum. Rather, it should be approached as one piece of an integrated strategy for enhancing access to the legal system by persons of limited means. Pro bono projects and programs are best developed as part of a coordinated effort to maximize the delivery of legal services to persons of limited means in the community. Bar associations should attempt to avoid duplication of efforts already undertaken by other legal services providers.

Finally, bar leaders are encouraged to call upon the expertise of lawyers and others in the community who work routinely with persons of limited means. Staff attorneys in legal services organizations are a tremendous resource for educating bar leaders about the legal issues affecting persons in low-income groups, and the gaps in service that exist. Likewise, representatives from social services organizations can provide a wealth of information about the needs, concerns and challenges facing low-income individuals and communities.

Pros

- ☞ An integrated strategy helps to focus planning on the big picture: enhancing access to the legal system for persons of limited means. It also brings a broader range of resources to the planning table, thus providing a more comprehensive approach to problem-solving.

- ☞ An integrated strategy helps to avoid unnecessary duplication of efforts and competition for resources.

Cons

- ☞ Coordinated planning can result in competing interests and agendas.
- ☞ Coordinated planning may delay the planning process.

Contacts

Washington State Access to Justice Board
Staff Contact: Joan Fairbanks, Coordinator (206) 727-8282
Volunteer Contact: Paul Stritmatter (360) 533-2710

Tennessee Bar Association
Staff Contact: Steve Xanthopoulos, Director, West Tennessee Legal Services, Inc. (901) 426-1311
Volunteer Contact: B. Riney Green (615) 244-5200

Minnesota State Bar Association
Staff Contact: Nancy Kleeman (612) 673-6331
Volunteer Contact: James L. Baillie (612) 347-7013

Examples

Plan for Delivery of Civil Legal Services to Low Income Persons in Washington State (Attachment 1-C)

Excerpts from Minnesota Report of the Joint Legal Services Access and Funding Commission (Attachment 1-D)

SECTION 1 ATTACHMENTS

[New rule 4-6.5 is added.]

RULE 4-6.5 VOLUNTARY PRO BONO PLAN

(a) Purpose. The purpose of the voluntary pro bono attorney plan is to increase the availability of legal service to the poor. The following operating plan has as its goal the improvement of the availability of legal services to the poor and the expansion of present pro bono legal service programs. The following operating plan shall be implemented to accomplish this purpose and goal.

(b) Standing Committee on Pro Bono Legal Service. The president-elect of The Florida Bar shall appoint a standing committee on pro bono legal service to the poor.

(1) The standing committee shall be composed of:

a. five members of the board of governors of The Florida Bar, one of whom shall be the chair or a member of the Access to the Legal System Committee of the Board of Governors;

b. five past or current directors of The Florida Bar Foundation;

c. one trial judge and one appellate judge;

d. two representatives of civil legal assistance providers;

e. two representatives from local and statewide voluntary bar associations;

f. two public members, one of whom shall be a representative of the poor;

g. the president or designee of the Board of Directors of Florida Legal Services, Inc.; and

h. one representative of the out-of-state practitioners' section of The Florida Bar.

(2) Responsibilities of the Standing Committee. The standing committee shall:

a. receive reports from circuit committees submitted on standardized forms developed by the standing committee;

b. review and evaluate circuit court pro bono plans;

c. beginning in the first year in which individual attorney pro bono attorney reports are due, submit an annual report as to the activities and results of the pro bono plan to the board of governors of The Florida Bar, The Florida Bar Foundation, and to the Supreme Court of Florida;

d. present to the board of governors of The Florida Bar and to the Supreme Court of Florida any suggested changes or modifications to the pro bono rules.

(c) Circuit Pro Bono Committees. There shall be one circuit pro bono committee in each of the judicial circuits of

Florida. In each judicial circuit the chief judge of the circuit, or the chief judge's designee, shall appoint and convene the initial circuit pro bono committee and the committee shall appoint its chair.

(1) Composition of Circuit Court Pro Bono Committee. Each circuit pro bono committee shall be composed of:

a. the chief judge of the circuit or the chief judge's designee;

b. to the extent feasible, one or more representatives from each voluntary bar association, including each federal bar association, recognized by The Florida Bar and one representative from each pro bono and legal assistance provider in the circuit, which representatives shall be nominated by the association or provider; and

c. at least one public member and at least one client-eligible member, which members shall be nominated by the other members of the circuit pro bono committee.

Governance and terms of service shall be determined by each circuit pro bono committee. Replacement and succession members shall be appointed by the chief judge of the circuit or the chief judge's designee, upon nomination by the association, the provider organization or the circuit pro bono committee, as the case may be, as deemed appropriate or necessary to ensure an active circuit pro bono committee in each circuit.

(2) Responsibilities of Circuit Pro Bono Committee. The circuit pro bono committee shall:

a. prepare in written form a circuit pro bono plan after evaluating the needs of the circuit and making a determination of present available pro bono services;

b. implement the plan and monitor its results;

c. submit an annual report to The Florida Bar standing committee;

d. to the extent possible, current legal assistance and pro bono programs in each circuit shall be utilized to implement and operate circuit pro bono plans and provide the necessary coordination and administrative support for the circuit pro bono committee;

e. to encourage more lawyers to participate in pro bono activities, each circuit pro bono plan should provide various support and educational services for participating pro bono attorneys, which, to the extent possible, should include:

1. providing intake, screening, and referral of prospective clients;

2. matching cases with individual attorney expertise, including the establishment of specialized panels;

3. providing resources for litigation and out-of-pocket expenses for pro bono cases;

4. providing legal education and training for pro bono attorneys in specialized areas of law useful in providing pro bono legal service;

5. providing the availability of consultation with attorneys who have expertise in areas of law with respect to which a volunteer lawyer is providing pro bono legal service;

6. providing malpractice insurance for volunteer pro bono lawyers with respect to their pro bono legal service;

7. establishing procedures to ensure adequate monitoring and follow-up for assigned cases and to measure client satisfaction; and

8. recognition of pro bono legal service by lawyers.

(f) The following are suggested pro bono service opportunities that should be included in each circuit plan:

1. representation of clients through case referral;

2. interviewing of prospective clients;

3. participation in pro se clinics and other clinics in which lawyers provide advice and counsel;

4. acting as co-counsel on cases or matters with legal assistance providers and other pro bono lawyers;

5. providing consultation services to legal assistance providers for case reviews and evaluations;

6. participation in policy advocacy;

7. providing training to the staff of legal assistance providers and other volunteer pro bono attorneys;

8. making presentations to groups of poor persons regarding their rights and obligations under the law;

9. providing legal research;

10. providing guardian ad litem services;

11. providing assistance in the formation and operation of legal entities for groups of poor persons; and

12. serving as a mediator or arbitrator at no fee to the client-eligible party.

Original Proceeding - Rules Regulating The Florida Bar and Rules of Judicial Administration

Talbot D'Alemberte and Randall C. Berg, Jr. of Steel, Hector & Davis, Miami, Florida,

for Petitioner

Alan T. Dimond, President, The Florida Bar, Miami, Florida; Patricia A. Seitz, President-elect, The Florida Bar, Miami, Florida; John F. Harkness, Jr., Executive Director, The Florida Bar, Tallahassee, Florida; James A. Baxter, Clearwater, Florida; Mary Ellen Bateman, UPL Counsel, The Florida Bar, Tallahassee, Florida; Alan R. Schwartz, Chief Judge, Third District Court of Appeal, Miami, Florida; Joseph W. Little, Gainesville, Florida; Harvey M. Alper, Altamonte Springs, Florida; Michael H. Davidson, Tallahassee, Florida; and J. Marion Moorman, Public Defender, Polk County Courthouse, Bartow, Florida,

Responding

William A. VanNortwick, Jr., Chair, Jacksonville, Florida; and Paul C. Doyle, Staff Director, Orlando, Florida, on behalf of the Report of The Florida Bar/Florida Bar Foundation Joint Commission on the Delivery of Legal Services to the Indigent in Florida.

WSBA LEGAL AID COMMITTEE

VOLUNTEER ATTORNEY LEGAL SERVICES ACTION PLAN

INTRODUCTION

In May, 1992, the Washington State Bar Association resolved that each member should contribute "public interest legal service" to low income persons or to matters designed primarily to address the needs of the low income individual in the state. The WSBA Legal Aid Committee was charged with developing an action plan for the implementation of this resolution.

To begin the development of this plan, the Committee, with the cooperation of Chief Justice Andersen, hosted the Volunteer Attorney Legal Services (VALS) Action Plan Conference in April 15, 1994 in Seattle. The conference was attended by representatives of the judiciary, law firms, law schools, bar leaders, volunteer legal service providers, members of legal services funding sources and WSBA officers and staff.

The result is now presented to the WSBA Board of Governors for its approval and implementation. This plan has developed strategies for every facet of the legal community to remove barriers which make it difficult for attorneys to provide volunteer legal services and to encourage attorneys to provide these services.

It is the hope of all those participating in the conference that the resulting plan will have a significant impact on the citizens of Washington state and their ability to achieve access to justice.

I. RECRUITMENT

Encouraging the individual attorney to choose to volunteer is essential to a more widespread commitment in Washington to VALS. The following strategies are intended to overcome some obstacles to that choice, such as availability of malpractice insurance or the fact that an individual attorney's specialty may not be relevant to local needs. More importantly, however, they include a set of institutional incentives to encourage individuals to decide to perform volunteer legal work. Some institutions (such as the judiciary) are asked to use their prestige to educate and recruit volunteer attorneys; other are asked to incorporate incentives into their structure that encourage their employees or members to perform VALS work.

JUDICIARY

A. Letter from the local bench prepared for all attorneys in the county which mentions oath and code of ethics section that attorneys should render VALS.

B. Develop better coordination between judges and VALS coordinators to identify attorneys willing to do VALS.

1. VALS coordinators share the lists that they have developed of VALS in their respective service areas with the bench.

2. Investigate small counties to determine whether the need exists for a list.

3. Encourage judges to assist local coordinator to recruit volunteer attorneys.

C. Judges should encourage VALS coordinator/board members to attend all swearing-in ceremonies for the new lawyers.

PRIVATE LAW FIRMS

A. Within each law firm, the firm should develop and publicize policies, strategies, and commentaries on law firm's mechanisms for encouraging attorneys in firm to do VALS.

WSBA

A. WSBA should adopt and market a volunteer attorney legal services challenge program for all law firms comparable to the ABA Law Firm Pro Bono Challenge.

1. Develop law firm volunteer attorney legal services challenge for Washington.

2. Market volunteer attorney legal services challenge.

3. As soon as a law firm accepts challenge, WSBA should contact the VALS coordinators in the areas where law firm practices about acceptance.

4. WSBA should gather data on success of program annually and publicize the firms that implement the challenge.

B. WSBA should collect representative VALS policies and manuals used by private firms; develop model law firm VALS policies and distribute these models.

C. As a part of the new ethics MCLE requirement of six hrs. of ethics continuing education every three years. CLEs should include a.) discussion of an attorney's professional responsibility to provide VALS work; b.) all appropriate CLEs should provide information on how to fulfill your professional VALS responsibility in that field of law.

D. Assist local VALS coordinators with recruitment.

1. Tear-out pages in the *Bar News* that both recruit and provide lists of supportive resources.

2. Develop similar recruitment inserts to be published in local and specialty bar newsletters and the *Washington Journal.*

LOCAL BAR ASSOCIATIONS

A. CLEs by local bar associations (accredited by MCLE Board) could provide free CLE credits to attorneys in exchange for a certain number of hours of VALS.

B. Monitor local participation in VALS and assist local VALS coordinators in recruitment.

LAW SCHOOLS

A. Education about the professional responsibility and need for VALS in the law schools.

1. Invite WSBA members to speak at orientation of law students, ethics and in relevant classes about VALS responsibility.

2. Each law school should develop a program where law students are encouraged to participate in VALS, including assistance to attorneys on VALS cases.

VALS COORDINATORS

A. Prepare booklet with local focus; names and phone numbers for program; what VALS program does and how to get involved.

II. SUPPORT TO VALS

Once individuals have chosen to perform VALS work, making certain informational, institutional, and financial resources easily available will support the effective delivery of legal services. Just as important, it will facilitate a continued commitment to volunteer work. Some attorneys face particular barriers, such as those in government and in-house counsel positions, whose employers may be less willing or able to provide the nonlegal support necessary or helpful to effective volunteer representative. Others may face major informational obstacles, such as a lack of knowledge or experience in the subject areas in which volunteer legal work is needed. The following strategies are designed to overcome these types of obstacles and provide continuing support to individuals performing VALS.

JUDICIARY

A. Minimize disincentives associated with delays on court calendars while handling a VALS case. Local benches implement mechanisms to facilitate prompt hearings for VALS cases which do not single out low income people by identifying their status nor unduly disadvantage those clients that pay attorneys for services.

1. Superior Court Judges Association investigate the mechanisms used in other states to accomplish this goal and consult with representatives of the affected parties about these mechanisms.

2. Then the Association will develop a variety of effective mechanisms which the local benches can chose from to effectuate this goal.

WSBA

A. Address the barrier that lack of malpractice coverage creates for many VALs attorneys, including retired, academic, in-house, and government lawyers. Possible source of such insurance would be NLADA which already writes such coverage for VALS programs in Snohomish and Pierce counties.

B. Develop a model for a complete family law resource center to be located in each county.

1. Model would include a triage for clients as they contact the resource center.

2. Center would coordinate with the local legal services program, VALS coordinator and mediation services to identify services for each client.

C. Develop a central resource clearinghouse to support attorneys who provide VALS which will provide information on VALS opportunities and supportive resources.

1. Compile list of a) local VALS programs b) local legal services programs c) current information on education and training programs available on VALS topics d) where and how mentors are available e) house a forms bank and f) maintain lists of ancillary services such as interpreters.

2. Create a VALS Deskbook with text and forms to go with high volume legal service type cases.

D. Continue and enhance the annual conference for VALS

E. The Board of Governors suggest that the MCLE Board consider whether to establish guidelines by which someone acting as a mentor could receive CLE credit (e.g. one CLE credit for every 2 hours of mentoring/learning, as reported by mentor, with a five-hour cap per year) and adopt such guidelines if feasible.

LOCAL VALS PROGRAMS

A. Develop a mentoring program to support VALS attorneys in areas of practice which are new to them.

1. Local VALS programs, both coordinators and board members, identify mentors by topics of expertise.

2. Have a mentor list with names and phone numbers to give new/solo attorneys.

3. Build from above to "mentor" programs to include advanced training form banks and on-going technical assistance.

B. Develop CLEs to train attorneys in "new" areas of law to encourage assistance in poverty law or specialty areas where there are not enough lawyers to aid the clients.

C. Locate supportive services to allow more attorneys to do VALS.

1. VALS coordinators and board members identify retired judges and offer to provide to them paralegal/typing resources to represent clients.

2. Identify and maintain lists of lay people who are willing to provide free services to facilitate VALS work, i.e. translators, legal secretaries, court reporters, expert witnesses, and professionals to perform needed evaluations.

GOVERNMENT, IN-HOUSE AND ACADEMIC LAWYERS

A. Make time and support services available to government attorneys to provide volunteer legal services.

   1. Ask government authorities to adopt policies on volunteerism by government employees, including their attorney employees.

   2. Liberalize leave time policies for government attorneys who wish to participate.

   3. Establish a private fund to purchase support such as secretarial services for VALS government attorneys.

B. Create partnership between government, in-house and academic lawyers and private law firms to provide staff and skills support.

   1. Private firms and corporate attorneys could provide conference room, computer use, and clerical support for government and academic attorneys who cannot use their office resources.

   2. Private attorneys can co-counsel with government, academic, and in-house counsel to help avoid malpractice and conflicts and identify areas of practice for VALS.

   3. Encourage corporations to consider VALS by their in-house staff to be part of the charitable contributions of the corporations.

   4. Encourage corporations to accept VALS Law Firm Challenge and to ask their outside counsel to do the same.

III. EFFECTIVE DELIVERY OF LEGAL SERVICES

An important VALS goal is to ensure that populations in need of legal services are served as effectively and efficiently as possible by volunteer attorneys. Individual energies and resources should be targeted toward the neediest groups. In order to maximize sharing of information about legal needs, avoid duplication of efforts, and make sure legal problems are addressed effectively, a wide variety of institutions involved in legal services – including VALS attorneys, paid legal services providers, the courts, and other dispute resolution centers – should regularly coordinate and pool information resources.

The following strategies also focus on delivery to "special populations," including individuals such as those in prisons and mental institutions, the homeless, the elderly, and those facing language barriers. Individuals in these groups may have only a limited awareness of their legal rights and resources. Moreover, their issues may often be better addressed by community resources such as counseling. Effective delivery of volunteer legal services may thus require special training of attorneys and may involve individuals other than attorneys to educate and assist these groups.

JUDICIARY

A. Consider feasibility of a limited practice license for non-WSBA attorneys to provide VALS and, if feasible, then expand Rule 9 to include non-WSBA member attorneys in government, in-house, and academic positions.

WSBA

A. Establish an effective link between volunteer attorney efforts and high priority legal needs.

   1. Identify and publicize firms that accept the VALS challenge.

   2. WSBA develop staff capacity to make referrals for both potential clients and volunteer attorneys to local VALs coordinators.

B. Identify and create opportunities to volunteer for government attorneys, lawyers that do not currently practice in an area relevant to local needs and enable non-WSBA attorneys to participate in:

   1. Advice clinics

   2. Mediation programs

   3. Self-help clinics

   4. Representation in administrative tribunals

5. Other non-litigation services

C. Approach ADR Section of the Bar to work in conjunction with WSBA to establish voluntary mediation panel for lawyers to serve as volunteers for low income clients on local basis and train these lawyers on mediation.

D. Develop a resources pool of experts and materials on special populations.

1. WSBA influence local bars to establish interested lawyer groups committed to special population issues.

2. WSBA establish on a computer network the resources state-wide that have been identified on a local level as resources available to assist in serving special populations.

3. Identify and provide needed training for VALS to provide services to an identified special population. Include written training materials in central resource clearinghouse described above in II. Support to VALS.

4. WSBA should tailor any of its pamphlets on legal rights to include the unique interests and concerns of the state's special populations.

LOCAL BAR ASSOCIATIONS

A. Identify and provide needed training for VALS to provide services to an identified special population. Also, identify and make available written materials on representing and being sensitive to the attitudes and culture of these special populations with the assistance of WSBA.

B. Local bar associations develop a community inventory of services that can support VALS needs, e.g.: YMCA, community colleges, interpreters, law schools, AIDS society, homeless shelters. Then coordinate these lists with those maintained by the local VALS coordinators.

PRIVATE LAW FIRMS

A. Law firms adopt a "clinic" that represents special population groups then serve as mentors to other lawyers on specific topics of concern to this population.

LOCAL VALS PROGRAMS

A. Regularly address local bar associations on volunteer opportunities in priority areas.

B. Coordinate efforts in making presentations to firms and to develop a plan for implementation of a firm's VALS commitment.

C. Develop a community inventory of services that can support VALS needs and coordinate this inventory with the local bar's inventory of these services. Develop computer system to keep this information current.

IV. RECOGNITION

As essential as recruitment, recognition represents further encouragement to the individual that chooses to perform VALS work. It also publicizes VALS and will encourage new recruits. The following strategies represent ways in which different institutions can recognize individuals that have donated their time and effort to performing volunteer legal services.

JUDICIARY

A. Ceremonies/events that involve judges with input from VALS coordinators.

B. All judicial associations develop mechanisms to give recognition to VALS.

PRIVATE LAW FIRMS

A. Each law firm develop appropriate mechanisms to recognize their attorneys' provision of VALS, such as an annual Honor Roll, recognition luncheon and/or other perks.

WSBA

A. Establish an annual Access To Justice Conference to recognize and support VALS.

B. Monthly WSBA Bar News column:

1. Snapshots-county by county recognition.

2. How to - very basic, practice tips.

3. Remind attorneys of professional responsibility and need for VALS.

Local Bar Associations

A. Work with local VALS coordinators to develop creative and meaningful ways to recognize the VALS contributions of local attorneys.

V. FUNDING

The success of current VALS programs and the ability of those programs to expand is directly linked to adequate funding for staff, office expenses, materials and other program costs. WSBA, local bar associations, legal service providers, VALS programs, the Legal Foundation of Washington and other parties concerned about VALS programs must work to assure current levels of funding and to develop additional funding to offset inflation and provide for expansion of VALS programs to serve unmet needs.

ACCESS TO JUSTICE BOARD

2001 Sixth Avenue, Suite 500 • Seattle, WA 98121-2599
Phone: (206) 727-8282 Fax: (206) 727-8320

EQUAL JUSTICE FOR ALL

October 20, 1995

Dear Colleague:

Enclosed please find a copy of the "Plan for Delivery of Civil Legal Services to Low Income Persons in Washington State," adopted by the Access to Justice Board at its October 13, 1995 meeting. This Plan is Section VII. of the overall State Service Delivery Plan to be submitted to the Legal Services Corporation on November 1, 1995. The Legal Services Corporation will utilize this plan as a guide in making decisions regarding LSC funding in Washington State. Sections I. through VI. are still in draft form and not yet available for distribution. They will provide LSC with a more in-depth discussion of the ATJ Board and its mission; the history of the legal services delivery system in our state; specifics on current funding for legal services; a description of the legal services and voluntary legal services providers; and an overview of circumstances giving rise to the need to restructure the delivery system.

The ATJ Board will now turn its attention to the details involved in implementing the Plan. The Board will continue to keep you apprised of developments in the Statewide Planning Project, and welcomes your continued participation. The next ATJ Board meeting is November 17, 1995 from 9 a.m. to 5 p.m. at the Washington State Bar Association in Seattle. **Please let us know by November 13 if you plan to attend.**

On behalf of the ATJ Board, I want to thank all the stakeholders who have made presentations, submitted comments, attended our meetings, and otherwise contributed to what has been to date an extremely valuable and productive process in the face of unprecedented attacks on legal services for the poor and extremely tight deadlines. We are very fortunate to have many leaders in our access to justice community who possess a positive and creative vision for a client-centered delivery system, and who "refuse to lose" sight of the goal of access to justice for all.

Very truly yours,

Paul L. Stritmatter

Paul L. Stritmatter
Chair

enclosure

Established by the Washington State Supreme Court
Administered by the Washington State Bar Association

vii. Plan for Delivery of Civil Legal Services to Low Income Persons in Washington State

The Access to Justice Board has adopted a philosophy regarding the delivery of civil legal services to low income people. Embodied in the document entitled "Visioning Justice: Hallmarks of an Effective Statewide Civil Legal Services Delivery System," (Hallmarks) this philosophy is based on notions of fundamental fairness and the rule of law. It declares that the mission of Washington state's civil legal services delivery system is to:

* Protect the individual rights of low income clients;

* Employ the civil justice system to oppose laws, regulations, policies and practices that operate unfairly against low income individuals and groups;

* Promote the interests of low income individuals and groups in the development and implementation of laws, regulations, policies and practices that directly affect their quality of life;

* Employ a broad range of legal advocacy approaches to expand the legal rights of low income individuals and groups where to do so is consistent with considerations of fundamental fairness and dignity; and

* Empower low income individuals and groups to understand and effectively assert their legal rights and interests within the civil justice system, with or without the assistance of legal counsel.

BACKGROUND

The Access to Justice Board (ATJ Board) believes that this mission can be most effectively fulfilled through a unified statewide service delivery system. However, the current delivery system can no longer be maintained due to federal efforts to extend all federal funding conditions and restrictions to private and other public funds received by federally-funded legal services providers. Under all legislative scenarios, these restrictions will attach to all funds -- IOLTA, state, local, public and private -- received by federal Legal Services Corporation (LSC) grantees effective January 1, 1996.

These federal restrictions will limit the nature, substance and scope of client representation, as well as who can receive legal services, in ways that are fundamentally inconsistent with the values and core capacities identified in the Hallmarks. Attachment A. They will interfere with professional decision making at many levels, undermine the ability of legal services attorneys to effectively represent their clients, and deny to legal services clients attorneys who can provide a full range of legal representation in the forums most appropriate to the clients' cases. Substantial relevant client representation will continue to be allowed under new federal guidelines, and LSC funds should continue to be part of the overall effort to fund equal justice activities in our state. But, application of these federal restrictions to all funds renders the current federally-funded programs incapable of providing a full range of client services consistent with the articulated mission; and this is the impetus to reconfigure the current delivery system.

STRUCTURAL CHANGE

The Access to Justice Board determines it necessary and appropriate to recommend a restructuring of the civil legal services delivery system to strategically use non-federal funds to complement client representational activities underwritten with federal funds. The goal is to ensure continuing capacity of the system as a whole (i.e., staffed programs, volunteer attorney programs, law school clinics, other direct service providers, etc.) to provide a full range of legal services to the broadest spectrum of clients in need, consistent with the Hallmarks.

The ATJ Board recommends the creation of two separate but complementary statewide legal services programs operating in service of the common mission outlined in the Hallmarks. One program, as yet unidentified, will be the recipient of LSC funds; the other -- the statewide successor to the three existing legal services programs -- will provide legal services using non-LSC funds. Each program will utilize in-house staff and private attorneys to ensure continuity in the availability of a full range of civil legal services to low income clients throughout the state of Washington within the scope of, and limitations on, their respective resources.

STATEWIDE LSC-GRANTEE

The ATJ Board recommends that LSC award 1996 funds to a single statewide grantee. This grantee will use 1996 LSC funds to establish and maintain a statewide staffed service delivery presence and to assume primary responsibility for providing financial, staff and technical support to the state's local volunteer attorney programs. This grantee must meet numerous requirements as described in Attachment B, The Legal Services Corporation Request for Proposals, 1996, pp. 18 - 21. In addition, this program will serve as the primary client entry point into the legal services delivery system; employing existing and emerging technologies to expand and integrate intake, case screening and case referral capacities to serve all primary service delivery components of the system.

In the period between now and January 1, 1996, the three existing legal services programs should assist in the development and initial staffing of this program, and timely transfer of pending client cases that can be handled consistent with federal funding restrictions and ethical considerations.

As the establishment of this new statewide provider moves forward, the access to justice community should understand that this is a period of transition. Not all necessary tasks can be accomplished at once, and major tasks must be split into viable and manageable steps. The ATJ

Board encourages the community to continue to assess what further organizational consolidations might be appropriate as we go through this transition.

CONSOLIDATION OF LEGAL SERVICES PROGRAMS OF WASHINGTON

The Access to Justice Board recommends that the boards of directors of Evergreen Legal Services, Puget Sound Legal Assistance Foundation, and Spokane Legal Services Center take action to consolidate these three programs into a single statewide legal services program. (This program can be named as the boards desire, but will be referred to in this document as "Columbia Legal Services".) Columbia Legal Services should receive local and state funds, including IOLTA funds, and is charged with maintaining those core capacities not able to be carried forward by the federally funded legal services provider, including, but not limited to, providing relevant client services to distinct and disproportionately disadvantaged statewide client populations (e.g., migrant agricultural workers, Native Americans, senior citizens, residents of juvenile, correctional and long term care facilities, etc.); accepting referrals of cases from the federally funded provider or other LSC-funded service providers, where the nature of the advocacy required (i.e., class actions, legislative or administrative advocacy, challenges to constitutionality of statutes, welfare reform cases, etc.) falls outside of the range of activities allowed under federal restrictions; developing and making available to the legal services community supplemental private bar capacity to handle cases that, because of federal restrictions, the federally funded provider or private attorneys working in association with that program cannot handle; and providing statewide support, litigation assistance, technical assistance, and training to all components of the statewide civil legal services delivery system -- both restricted and unrestricted.

VOLUNTEER ATTORNEY LEGAL SERVICES

Volunteer Attorney Legal Services (VALS) programs are partners with direct service programs in providing access to justice for low income people throughout Washington. These programs, along with the statewide federally funded provider and Columbia Legal Services and the larger equal justice community, face several key tasks to preserve and expand this partnership. They must ensure sufficient funding for future operation, maintain effective lines of communication with local bar members and other local stakeholders during this time of major change, develop viable mechanisms that allow VALS programs a coordinated statewide voice, and assess other possible service delivery mechanisms, e.g., regional intake, screening, and referral. Because VALS programs are smaller entities and face survival problems if funding levels sink too low, development of an adequate funding base is essential. The ATJ Board recommends that VALS programs be given assurance that grant levels will be maintained at, or near, 1995 IOLTA/LSC grant levels, at least through 1996 to ensure continued operation of VALS programs, regardless of the actual funding source.

The ATJ Board recognizes that some current private bar volunteer attorney program activities will not be able to be underwritten with LSC funds. These activities should be identified and segregated from the LSC-funded volunteer attorney program(s), and transferred to a non-LSC funded entity in a manner that preserves the capacity of the private bar program(s) to maintain core services and, where appropriate, independent local identification.

LAW SCHOOL CLINICS

The ATJ Board believes that the current crisis also presents opportunities and imperatives for the state's three law schools and their respective clinical legal programs. As providers of additional needed client services, the law school clinical programs should be integrated into the overall service delivery system. The dialogue between the equal justice community and the law school clinical programs should continue, but refocus on opportunities to integrate the pedagogic needs of law students and high priority unmet legal needs of our state's low income residents.

STANDARDS

The Hallmarks adopted by the ATJ Board apply to all providers. Client representation provided by all components of the legal services delivery system (e.g., staffed full-service legal services programs, other direct service providers, VALS programs, law school clinics), should strive to meet the Rules of Professional Conduct, and other applicable professional standards including, but not limited to, the ABA Standards for the Delivery of Civil Legal Services to the Poor (1986), and the emerging ABA Standards for Programs Providing Civil Pro Bono Legal Services to Persons of Limited Means.

OTHER FUNDING SOURCES

The impending changes in federal funding amounts and the nature and scope of federal restrictions, and the ATJ Board's decision to recommend the establishment of two statewide legal services providers, will have logical implications for other entities which provide funding and support for civil legal services in Washington State. The ATJ Board is sensitive to independent decision making prerogatives of these other funding entities, such as the Legal Foundation of Washington, regional Area Agencies on Aging, local United Ways, LAW Fund, etc. Nevertheless, the Board believes it appropriate to make recommendations to these entities as part of its overall recommendations relating to the reconfiguration of our state's civil legal services delivery system.

Because the state filing fee funds are a resource that, at this time, even with current restrictions allows flexible representation and does not affect the integrity of the unrestricted funds, the ATJ Board recommends that legislatively appropriated state funding be directed to Columbia Legal Services. The ATJ Board further recommends that restrictive language that undermines the Hallmarks be eliminated and that the statutory commitment of these funds for specific categories of cases be removed. Columbia Legal Services must be free to provide services consistent with the needs of clients, rather than on the basis of artificial legislatively decided substantive case priorities.

The ATJ Board recommends that IOLTA funding in 1996 be directed to support the activities of Columbia Legal Services and such other client service providers that demonstrate both the practical need to maintain a separate identity and the irreconcilability of their primary activities with federal restrictions. A similar recommendation is made with respect to other renewable non-

LSC funds currently received by the three existing legal services programs (e.g., CDBG, United Way, LAW Fund, Older Americans Act, etc.).

RESOURCE DEVELOPMENT

In light of the federal retreat from historic equal justice funding commitments, the Access to Justice Board acknowledges the critical need to develop new and expanded financial resources to support equal justice activities now and into the future. In this area, the ATJ Board recommends that the new LPO rule be aggressively implemented, and that all entities presently working to expand funding for civil legal services in our state (i.e., LAW Fund, local bar associations and bar foundations, the Legal Foundation of Washington, the Equal Justice Coalition, etc.), work cooperatively to expand the resource base to the benefit of the entire service delivery network.

BEYOND 1996

This is a time for large reductions in legal services staffing. This is also a time of change for other providers in the access to justice community. As a result, it is difficult to make specific commitments beyond 1996 to the continuation of all of the activities discussed in this report. Clarity about the extended future of the delivery of civil legal services to the poor in Washington state will emerge as we proceed through this time of transition. The foregoing recommendations are adopted in contemplation of pending federal legislation and will be revisited if the final legislation is substantially different than what was contemplated.

Having provided an overview and explanation of the Board's thinking, the Access to Justice Board recommends the following.

SPECIFIC RECOMMENDATIONS FOR WASHINGTON'S STATE PLAN

1. A new statewide legal services entity, established separate and apart from the three legal services programs of Washington, bid for 1996 federal funds. This entity will provide client services on a statewide basis, proposing the deployment of staff and private bar capacity and institutional integration into a comprehensive statewide legal services delivery system that is consistent with the principles and values articulated in the Hallmarks.

2. The Legal Services Corporation award 1996 Basic Field, Migrant and Native American funding to an entity that commits to providing statewide services consistent with the foregoing structure.

3. The designated LSC-provider establish a grantor-grantee relationship with local Volunteer Attorney Legal Services (VALS) programs whose primary activities are consistent with emerging federal funding restrictions; and a primary component of this provider's Private Attorney Involvement plan be to underwrite the operational costs of, and provide technical assistance to, such local volunteer attorney programs.

4. The ATJ Board recommends that VALS programs be given assurance that grant levels will be maintained at, or near, 1995 IOLTA/LSC grant levels, at least through 1996 to ensure continued operation of VALS programs, regardless of the actual funding source.

5. The legal services and volunteer attorney community identify volunteer attorney program components and other PAI activities that are likely to be inconsistent with federal funding restrictions (which are anticipated to accompany subgrant funding), and develop alternative institutional structures and capacity on state, regional and/or local level to ensure the continuing ability of volunteer attorneys to pursue essential client representation in conjunction with programs that are fiscally segregated from federally funded legal services programs.

6. The boards of directors of Evergreen Legal Services, Puget Sound Legal Assistance Foundation, and Spokane Legal Services Center consolidate these existing LSC-funded programs into a single statewide program which maintains the full range of core capacities outlined in the Hallmarks, and which works in partnership with the federal funds recipient to develop common state, regional and local client needs assessments and service delivery plans, and to develop and implement integrated client intake, brief service, referral, and case handling capacity. This consolidated program should be responsible for:

* Enforcing civil and individual rights of clients through effective advocacy in all appropriate forums;

* Continuity of services to migrant farmworkers,

residents of juvenile, corrections and long term care institutions, and Native American residents of the state;

* Identifying, developing and implementing plans to serve other client constituencies that are in need of specialized, focused representation;

* Legislative and administrative representation where necessary, appropriate and consistent with client needs;

* Class actions;

* Within the constraints of available resources, establishment of local, regional and statewide capacity to accept referrals and otherwise handle high priority cases that the federally-funded providers will be unable to handle;

* In consultation with appropriate volunteer attorney providers, develop, fund and otherwise support private attorney involvement initiatives designed to increase the delivery system's capacity to represent clients on matters restricted or prohibited under applicable federal rules.

* State support, training, and technical assistance to all persons involved in the delivery of legal services to low income clients, including staff of other federally and non-federally funded direct service providers, private volunteer attorneys, courthouse facilitators, etc.

7. The equal justice community further explore opportunities to integrate non-LSC funded direct service providers into the consolidated statewide entity; provided that, where legitimate and compelling reasons exist to preserve separate program identities, the equal justice community should be prepared to act accordingly, and to maintain the relative capacity of such non-LSC direct service providers to provide legal services to eligible clients, to the extent that such services are consistent with the overall legal needs of clients and are delivered as part of the integrated service delivery system.

8. The LSC-grantee establish a grantor-grantee relationship between itself and other existing direct service providers the activities of which are anticipated to be substantially consistent with anticipated federal restrictions; provided that, where certain activities of existing non-LSC direct

service providers would be inconsistent with federal restrictions, but where the primary work undertaken by such providers is otherwise consistent with anticipated restrictions, capacity to engage in such non-conforming activities should be transferred to an appropriate non-federally funded legal services provider or office.

9. Both the LSC-grantee and Columbia Legal Services deploy staff and other resources on a generally proportional basis, with due regard given to the location of special populations, local and regional affinities, the availability of other local and regional resources, other relevant socio-geographic considerations, and the short-term need to maintain the greatest possible continuity of services to clients.

10. Where feasible, legal services providers and volunteer attorney programs utilize available and emerging technologies to establish local and regional intake, case screening and client referral systems that simultaneously serve all case handling components of the local or regional delivery system, and integrate specialty private bar providers into the intake and screening process.

11. To the extent authorized by state law, appropriated state funds be distributed to the consolidated statewide non-federally funded program (Columbia Legal Services).

12. The Legal Foundation of Washington distribute IOLTA funds to Columbia Legal Services and, where consistent with client needs, existing and projected case handling responsibilities, and other relevant criteria, to other appropriate service programs which are substantially engaged in activities that cannot be supported with federally-restricted dollars.

13. To ensure continuity of client services and minimize unnecessary administrative costs, the equal justice community encourage continuity of existing relationships between other public and private non-federal funding sources (e.g., LAW Fund, local community development block grants, city and county general funds, funds made available under the Older American Act, United Way funds, etc.) and Columbia Legal Services.

14. Where possible, law school clinical and pro bono service activities be refocused and expressly integrated into the overall client needs-driven statewide civil legal services delivery system.

15. Within the constraints imposed by the overall level and mix of available funding, personnel, and private bar resources, the legal services delivery community utilize existing and emerging technologies to provide expansive geographic coverage and maximize local legal services delivery capacity and presence in areas outside of principal urban centers.

16. The equal justice community aggressively pursue additional state funding to make up for the service capacity losses resulting from federal funding reductions, and also aggressively seek to remove from state enabling legislation (RCW 43.08.250, .250) language incorporating all federal restrictions by reference and language limiting the categories of cases that can be handled with state funds appropriated pursuant to the authority contained in those sections.

17. Resources be committed to maximize the timely implementation of the Supreme Court's rule requiring Limited Practice Officers to establish IOLTA-type accounts for the deposit of short term funds received in association with real and personal property closing services.

18. LAW Fund and other legal services-related entities (local bar associations and foundations, VALS programs, other direct service providers) engaged in fund raising work cooperatively in a common effort to maximize the total number of dollars raised and made available for equal justice activities undertaken through the integrated statewide civil legal services delivery system.

EXCERPTS

REPORT OF THE JOINT LEGAL SERVICES ACCESS AND FUNDING COMMITTEE

December 31, 1995

Every person is entitled to a certain remedy in the laws for all injuries or wrongs which he may receive in his person, property or character, and to obtain justice freely and without purchase, completely and without denial, promptly and without delay, conformable to the laws. (Minnesota Constitution, Art. I, Sec. 8)

INTRODUCTION

The 1995 session of the Minnesota Legislature directed the Minnesota Supreme Court to:

> [C]reate a joint committee including representatives from the Supreme Court, the Minnesota State Bar Association, and the Minnesota Legal Services Coalition to prepare recommendations for state funding changes or other alternatives to maintain an adequate level of funding and voluntary services that will address the critical civil legal needs of low-income persons as a result of reductions in federal government funding for such programs.

By Order dated September 21, 1995, the Minnesota Supreme Court established the Committee and directed it to:

> [E]xamine the alternatives for addressing the critical civil legal needs of low-income people including systemic changes in the legal and judicial systems and the legal services delivery system to facilitate access...identify[ing] costs and funding options for these alternatives and make recommendations to the Court and the Legislature by December 31, 1995.

The Court appointed 29 members to the Committee representing the Legislature, the federal and state judiciary, lawyers in private and public practice, legal services program staff, and the public.[1] The following 24 Committee members, and Supreme Court liaison Justice Edward Stringer, participated in the Committee's work:

Diane Ahrens
Gloria Bostic
Rep. Sherry Broecker
Patrick Burns
Leah Carpenter
Hon. Bruce Christopherson
Sen. Richard Cohen
Joseph Dixon
Glenn Dorfman
Daniel Gislason
Catharine Haukedahl
Jarvis Jones
Sen. David Knutson
Charles Krekelberg
David Kuduk
Bricker Lavik
William Mahlum
Barbara F.L. Penn, Co-chair
Steven Reyelts
Hon. James Rosenbaum
Mary Schneider
Jan Smaby
Roger Stageberg, Co-Chair
Hon. John Stanoch

At its first meeting on September 29, 1995, the Committee established subcommittees to identify issues and develop recommendations directed toward the court system, legal services programs and the private bar. Each subcommittee also reviewed funding issues and brought suggestions to the entire Committee to address.

The Committee understood its charge to include identifying both short-term and long-term solutions to meet the legal needs of low-income Minnesotans, especially in light of reductions in federal funding. In response to the question of how Minnesota's lawyers, the courts, and the Legislature can work together on this critical issue, the Committee adopted a **partnership approach** and focused on a **five year plan.**

---

[1] A complete listing of Committee members is in Appendix A. The Committee wishes to thank the staff of the Minnesota Supreme Court, the Minnesota State Bar Association and the legal services programs who assisted the Committee. The Committee also wishes to thank the Otto Bremer Foundation, which provided funding for the preparation and printing of this report.

I. EXECUTIVE SUMMARY

There exists in Minnesota, as across the nation, a very serious unmet need for civil legal services for low-income persons. Many organizations have documented this need including the American Bar Association, the Minnesota State Bar Association (MSBA), the Minnesota Supreme Court Gender Fairness Task Force, and the Minnesota Supreme Court Race Bias Task Force. Studies have consistently concluded that even the most critical legal needs -- such as those relating to housing, family income, and family violence -- are not adequately met. It is also clear that the work done by legal services programs

- stabilizes families, maintains communities and makes society safer;
- saves the taxpayers money;
- helps to prevent legal problems which would otherwise clog the court system; and
- helps people to become self-sufficient and participate effectively in society.

Federal funding for the national Legal Services Corporation (LSC) for 1996 is almost certain to be cut by 20-30 percent. While Congress had not completed action on the fiscal year 1996 appropriation as of December 31, 1995, it is also clear that Congress will impose numerous restrictions and prohibitions on the legitimate work that providers receiving federal funding can do for their clients. Other federal funding for legal services to senior citizens and persons with disabilities is also being cut approximately ten percent. This means a loss of over $1.7 million for Minnesota's programs. Some other funding sources such as local United Ways are also shrinking. At the same time, many laws affecting low-income Minnesotans are changing dramatically, creating new and additional legal needs.

Over 80 percent of the resources currently available to meet the critical legal needs of low-income Minnesotans come through the staff and volunteer lawyers who work with the six programs that serve all 87 Minnesota counties. The six programs work together as the Minnesota Legal Services Coalition (Coalition). The remainder of the resources come through a variety of other staffed offices and free-standing volunteer attorney programs generally providing additional services in single counties or to special populations. Collectively, Minnesota's legal services programs are considered nationwide as a model for the ways in which they have worked cooperatively with each other, the private bar, funders, the courts, and the Legislature. Unfortunately, additional efficiencies notwithstanding, decreased funding will inevitably result in decreased available services and in a greater unmet need for low-income Minnesotans.

The Committee explored issues facing, and developed recommendations directed toward, the court system, the legal services programs themselves, and the private bar. The Committee also developed recommendations for legislative action.

RECOMMENDATIONS[2]

With respect to the court system, the Committee recommends that:

A. Each judicial district should approve and implement an action plan to help meet the legal needs of low-income Minnesotans consistent with judicial ethical requirements.

B. Courts' efforts to improve services to pro se litigants should address the special needs of low-income users.

C. Trial judges in all courts in Minnesota should be educated about the need for funding for legal services for the disadvantaged, and be encouraged to consider making counsel and litigants aware of the possibility, in appropriate cases, of designating local legal services or volunteer programs, or the Supreme Court's Legal Services Advisory Committee (LSAC), as the recipients of cy pres funds. This is money left over after class action proceeds have been distributed as far as possible.

With respect to the legal services providers, the Committee recommends that:

A. While the Coalition programs and others are already a national model of coordination and cooperation, the programs should continue to search for areas in which they can achieve additional efficiencies and improve client services through increased coordination and cooperation.

B. All civil legal services providers should become familiar with and abide by the ABA's Standards for Providers of Civil Legal Services and, when available, the ABA's Standards for Pro Bono Providers.

C. LSAC and the Lawyer Trust Account Board (LTAB) should explore asking all legal services providers to use a common format for keeping track of and reporting case service statistics to facilitate monitoring and evaluation of the overall delivery of civil legal services to the poor in Minnesota.

D. Each local legal services provider should establish an administrative client fee or fees, which may be voluntary or mandatory at the option of the local program's board, in the suggested amount of at least $10, subject to hardship exceptions, and the programs should report to LSAC with respect to their ideas and experiences with such fees.

E. The legal services delivery system should continue to strive to offer to low-income people a level playing field, access to all forums and a full range of legal services in areas of critical need.

---

[2]This report reflects the views of the Joint Legal Services Access and Funding Committee. It does not necessarily reflect the views of the Minnesota Legislature, the Minnesota Supreme Court, the Minnesota State Bar Association, or any other organization or agency that had representation on the Committee.

F. Legal services funding should be structured to ensure that populations with special needs, such as Native Americans, migrant and seasonal farm workers, people with disabilities, and financially distressed family farmers, continue to have access to legal services and that adequate state support services, such as training, community legal education materials and mechanisms for information sharing, continue to be available to all legal services providers, including volunteer attorney programs.

With respect to the private bar, the Committee recommends that:

A. The organized bar and local legal services providers should encourage all lawyers to meet their obligation under revised Rule 6.1 to donate 50 hours of legal services annually, primarily to the disadvantaged, and to make direct financial contributions to local legal services providers.

B. Volunteer attorney programs should continue to be well funded so that there are adequate means at the local level to match client needs with volunteer lawyers. The MSBA should provide additional technical support to assist local programs with fundraising and increasing donated legal services.

C. The MSBA's Legal Assistance to the Disadvantaged Committee should be encouraged to develop a system for measuring the pro bono activities undertaken by Minnesota lawyers in order to establish a baseline for those activities, to encourage more lawyers to participate, and to evaluate whether efforts to increase such activity are successful.

D. The bar should encourage and support private fundraising initiatives undertaken by the legal services providers.

E. The MSBA and LTAB should work together to encourage Minnesota banks to restore the interest rates on lawyers' trust accounts to earlier levels. Even a one percent increase would substantially increase the revenue available for distribution to legal services programs.

F. To ensure that all lawyers assume an increased part of the responsibility for funding legal services providers, beyond the voluntary financial contributions that many individual lawyers already make, the Supreme Court should be petitioned to increase the annual lawyer registration fee by $50 for lawyers practicing more than three years, and $25 for lawyers practicing three years or less, with the increase going to the Legal Services Advisory Committee for allocation to legal services providers, including volunteer attorney programs.

With respect to the Legislature, the Committee requests that funds appropriated from the general fund for legal services be increased as follows:

•The appropriation base for civil legal services should be increased by $900,000 for the fiscal year which begins on July 1, 1996, bringing the annual base amount to $5,907,000.

•The appropriation base for civil legal services should be increased by $1,000,000 for the fiscal year which begins July 1, 1997, bringing the annual base amount to $6,907,000.

•The appropriation base for civil legal services should be increased by $1,500,000 for the fiscal year which begins on July 1, 1999, bringing the annual base amount to $8,407,000.

Because the Committee believes that providing access to civil justice for all people, like access to criminal justice, is a fundamental responsibility of our society, the Committee does not believe that appropriations should be increased only if a new revenue source is created. The Committee notes that the following revenue sources exist or could be created by the Legislature:

•The State has a projected surplus in the general fund in excess of $500,000,000.

•The fee for filing certain real estate documents could be increased by $2, as was done in 1992 and 1993. This would generate $1.8 million per fiscal year.

•The fee for filing civil court lawsuits could be increased by $8. This would generate $1.1 million per fiscal year.

•The annual filing fee for professional corporations could be increased by $75 per year. This would generate $290,000 per fiscal year.

The pros and cons regarding the use of each of the above sources are discussed in Section VII, below.

These increases, if implemented, will offset the current and pending 1996 LSC funding losses. If no further losses occur in the next few years, these increases would also significantly reduce the unmet need, which carries a serious cost to our State. They would also provide a stable funding base, leaving Minnesota's low-income citizens less vulnerable to the effects of unpredictable political changes on the national level. Additional means of addressing the unmet needs should also continue to be explored.

VI. RECOMMENDATIONS TO THE PRIVATE BAR

In Minnesota, the legal profession has a long tradition of providing uncompensated legal services to people who cannot afford them. Meaningful access to our system of justice usually requires the assistance of a lawyer. Minnesota lawyers, understanding that the disadvantaged must have access to justice, fill an important and expanding role in the overall delivery of legal services to the disadvantaged. Organized volunteer attorney programs, some of which are almost 30 years old, have continued to grow. LSC-funded programs are required to make an amount equal to 12.5 percent of their LSC grant available to provide opportunity for the involvement of private attorneys in the delivery of legal assistance to eligible clients. The pool of lawyers who volunteer their services through the structured programs in Minnesota has increased from under 500 in 1981 to over 3,000 in 1994.[15] The MSBA's Directory of Pro Bono Opportunities for Attorneys lists over 70 organizations through which lawyers can volunteer.[16] Unfortunately, as the need for legal services is increasing, the ability of LSC-funded and other programs to meet the need is adversely affected by shrinking resources and LSC restrictions. Volunteer lawyers will be increasingly called upon to help meet the legal service needs of the disadvantaged.

Recent efforts build upon many years of MSBA activity in support of access to legal services generally and volunteer legal services specifically. The MSBA encouraged and assisted with formation of volunteer attorney programs to serve all 87 Minnesota counties in the early 1980s. The MSBA's Director of Volunteer Legal Services provides technical assistance and support to Minnesota civil legal services providers including volunteer attorney programs. The MSBA has developed, adopted and disseminated Model Pro Bono Policies and Procedures for Law Firms and Government Attorneys. The MSBA's Legal Assistance to the Disadvantaged (LAD) Committee is currently circulating for comment a draft model pro bono policy for law schools. More broadly, the MSBA has consistently supported adequate funding for civil legal services delivery and has actively worked in the Legislature to encourage increased funding. In 1994, the MSBA led efforts to form Minnesotans for Legal Services, a broad-based organization whose mission is to ensure that people throughout Minnesota are kept informed about legal services developments in Washington and St. Paul so that they can advocate with members of Congress and the state Legislature in support of legal services.

---

[15] ABA 1994 Harrison Tweed Award Nominee Information Sheet for Minnesota State Bar Association, at p. 4.

[16] For additional history and description of pro bono in Minnesota, see McCaffrey, "Pro Bono in Minnesota: A History of Volunteerism in the Delivery of Civil Legal Services to Low Income Clients," Law & Inequality 13:77 (1994).

A. Rule 6.1. The organized bar and local legal services providers should encourage all lawyers to meet their obligation under revised Rule 6.1 to donate 50 hours of legal services annually, primarily to the disadvantaged, and to make direct financial contributions to local legal services providers.

To respond to the unmet need for legal services, Minnesota lawyers and their professional organizations recently have moved aggressively to increase the amount of voluntary legal services for the disadvantaged. The MSBA's petition to the Minnesota Supreme Court to amend Rule 6.1 of the Minnesota Rules of Professional Conduct was granted on December 11, 1995, to be effective on January 1, 1996. This Committee recommended that the Supreme Court adopt the MSBA's petition, and the Committee co-chairs submitted a letter to the Court conveying its support, before the Court's November 15, 1995 hearing on Rule 6.1.

The revisions strengthen the Rule by stating an aspirational goal of 50 hours of volunteer service per year, the substantial majority for the disadvantaged, and giving a clear definition which focuses on legal services to persons of limited means. The Rule also encourages lawyers to contribute money to legal services providers as well as donating volunteer time. The Committee supports the MSBA's LAD Committee in its plans for an extensive statewide educational campaign, in cooperation with local bar associations and local volunteer attorney programs, to acquaint lawyers with revised Rule 6.1 and to encourage them to comply with the aspirational goal. Written materials have already been prepared. The LAD Committee and MSBA staff will work with local programs on expanding the availability of volunteer legal services as well as on fundraising from individual private lawyers.

B. Strengthen Support for Volunteer Attorney Programs. Volunteer attorney programs should continue to be well funded so that there are adequate means at the local level to match client needs with volunteer lawyers. The MSBA should provide additional technical support to assist local programs with fundraising and increasing donated legal services.

1. Background

Organized volunteer attorney programs cover all 87 Minnesota counties. The structure in Minnesota that enables this effective and efficient involvement of the private bar is paid for in large part with LSC funds. Over 1,700 private lawyers donate legal services through the Coalition programs' volunteer and judicare programs, donating legal services valued well in excess of $3.5 million each year. These volunteer programs cover 78 of Minnesota's 87 counties. Volunteer lawyer services in the other nine counties are coordinated by five free-standing programs. While these organizations receive some funding from LSC grantees, they are managerially separate and obtain funding from other sources, such as LTAB, LSAC, county boards, and donations from local lawyers and law firms. These programs are Legal Assistance of Dakota County, Legal Assistance of Olmsted County, Legal Assistance of Washington County, Volunteer Attorney Program of Duluth, and Volunteer Lawyers Network. They are described in Appendix B.

For many years, private lawyers in Minnesota have also contributed financially to legal services providers. They now contribute approximately $500,000 each year through the SMRLS Campaign for Legal Aid, The Fund for the Legal Aid Society of Minneapolis, the Hennepin County Bar Association's Annual Bar Benefit and Volunteer Lawyers Network Silent Auction, the District 21 (Anoka County) Bar Association's and the Itasca Bar Association's annual giving, and other local fundraising activities.

The American Bar Association has issued a Pro Bono Challenge to the nation's 500 largest law firms, asking them to dedicate three to five percent of their billable hours annually to pro bono legal services, primarily to the disadvantaged. In Minnesota, 11 law firms, with approximately 1,000 lawyers, collectively, have accepted the Challenge. The Minnesota response is the highest percentage response in the country.

In addition to donating time and money, individual private lawyers also handle many cases at reduced fees for people whose incomes are slightly over the limits for free representation. If program funding is reduced and private attorneys are expected to fill the gap by doing more free work for the poor, this may put pressure on them to increase their fees for middle-income clients who already have difficulty affording representation. This could be especially true for small firms and solo practitioners, many in rural areas and many of whom are already under growing financial pressure.

Even before the creation of structured volunteer attorney programs, the bar acknowledged that its responsibilities included providing free legal services to people in need. Lawyers throughout Minnesota continue to provide such services directly as well as through the organized programs. It is difficult to determine how much service is provided informally. As law practice becomes more specialized and fewer lawyers engage in general practice, it may be more difficult for individuals needing free assistance to find a lawyer directly and organized volunteer programs may assume increased importance. Also, the organized programs provide a mechanism to ensure more equitable distribution of the uncompensated work, as well as a way to find representation for clients who approach a lawyer directly but whom that lawyer cannot assist. The organized programs provide lawyers with training in poverty law and the special needs of low-income clients, malpractice coverage for cases taken through the programs, mentors, and many other support services.

2. Steps to Strengthen Volunteer Attorney Programs.

Not only do low-income people need to be far better informed about their legal rights and about the availability of legal services, but the private bar, legislators, and the public also need to understand better the severity of the unmet need for low-income legal services, especially in areas beyond family and housing law. While many private lawyers already are contributing time, "in general, too few are asked to give too much. While they are surprisingly very successful in what they are able to accomplish, it is clear that they need [more] ... assistance."[17] Lawyers

[17] November 10, 1995, memo from Rep. Sherry Broecker to the Committee.

particularly need additional training on how to work effectively with low-income clients and in substantive poverty law. Even with the number of lawyers currently volunteering, there are some bottlenecks caused by insufficient staffing. As more lawyers volunteer more hours, considerable additional resources will be needed to screen the clients, match them with willing lawyers, and ensure that lawyers taking cases receive needed training and materials. In much of rural Minnesota, virtually every private lawyer is volunteering time already. In these areas, there are no more private lawyers to ask.

The Committee recommends that continued attention be given to the volunteer attorney programs to ensure that there is an adequate system to match the volunteer lawyers and the low-income clients. A portion of any increase in funding must be available to the volunteer attorney programs through which lawyers provide direct volunteer legal services to the poor.

Given the increase in critical legal needs and cuts in federal and other funding, the need for volunteer lawyers will increase. With the implementation of revised Rule 6.1, and continuing expansion of the ABA Pro Bono Challenge, the number of lawyers volunteering their time should also increase, as will the need to train and supervise volunteer lawyers and match them with clients. With some of the restrictions that Congress is imposing on the type of cases handled by LSC-funded programs, the disadvantaged who cannot be served by LSC programs will turn increasingly to the private lawyers. New approaches will need to be devised to engage more private lawyers in areas in which they have previously not routinely volunteered, for example, in complex litigation and public policy areas.

The Committee also recommends that the MSBA increase the resources it devotes to providing technical assistance to the volunteer attorney programs, as well as the other legal services providers. The MSBA, as a statewide organization of lawyers, is in a unique position to provide such support. This could include:

- improving approaches to fundraising from law firms and individual lawyers, especially by programs and in geographical areas in which this is not already being done.

- developing materials for programs to use in encouraging planned giving.

- encouraging law firms to place lawyers in fellowships with legal services providers for several months or for particular projects. This is sometimes known as rotation of volunteer lawyers or "lend-a-lawyer" and has been done successfully in several places around the country.

- assisting with grant proposals to community funds and foundations.

C. Reporting of Pro Bono. The MSBA's Legal Assistance to the Disadvantaged Committee should be encouraged to develop a system for measuring the activities undertaken by Minnesota lawyers in order to establish a baseline for that activity, to encourage more lawyers to participate, and to evaluate whether efforts to increase such activity are successful.

In 1990, the MSBA asked the Supreme Court to implement mandatory reporting of volunteer legal services and financial contributions to legal services providers. At that time, the Court issued an order strongly encouraging pro bono but declining to implement mandatory reporting. Since 1990, the Texas State Bar implemented voluntary reporting of pro bono and the New York State Bar conducted an extensive pro bono survey. Most recently, the Florida Supreme Court implemented mandatory reporting of pro bono time and financial contributions to legal services providers along with adoption of a rule similar to 6.1 setting an aspirational goal for pro bono hours or a specific dollar amount to be contributed in lieu of the hours. Since then, contributions of time and money have increased dramatically in Florida.

At the November 15, 1995, hearing on the MSBA's petition to amend Rule 6.1, the justices asked several questions about how the success of the revised rule might be measured and whether the MSBA had again considered the reporting of pro bono. Those questions were consistent with frustrations this Committee has experienced over the past four months. The Committee knows that a great deal of volunteer work is being done by lawyers in Minnesota, far in excess of the $3.5 million which is donated through the Coalition program volunteer components. However, it has proven impossible to come up with any reliable number. The Committee believes it is important that the Supreme Court, the Legislature, and the public have clear information on the extent to which lawyers in Minnesota are helping to address the unmet need for legal services. This Committee believes that the time is ripe to reconsider the idea of some form of reporting in Minnesota. The LAD Committee is in the best position to undertake such a review, consider the pros and cons of what has been done elsewhere, and recommend a process.

D. Private Fundraising Initiatives. The bar should encourage and support fundraising initiatives undertaken by the legal services providers.

Revised Rule 6.1 states that in addition to donating time, "a lawyer should voluntarily contribute financial support to organizations that provide legal services to persons of limited means." As noted above, Minnesota lawyers are already doing a great deal in this area. However, with increased need for services to the poor comes increased responsibility on lawyers to help meet that need. The Committee therefore recommends that all lawyers in Minnesota give increased encouragement and support to private fundraising initiatives by the legal services and volunteer attorney programs throughout the state.

E. **Lawyer Trust Account Interest. The MSBA and the Lawyer Trust Account Board should work together to encourage Minnesota banks to restore the interest rates on lawyers' trust accounts to earlier levels. Even a one percent increase would substantially increase the revenue available for distribution to legal services programs.**

As described in Section IIIA above, the MSBA, Minnesota banks, and the Supreme Court worked together in the early 1980s to create the Interest on Lawyers Trust Account program which is administered by the Lawyer Trust Account Board. The revenue available for LTAB grants has shrunk by over 50 percent in the past four years largely due to the fall in interest rates. Interest rates paid by banks on IOLTA accounts on December 31, 1995 are approximately 20 percent of what they were in 1987, while the prime rate charged by banks is 105 percent of what it was in 1987.[18] In 1993, most Minnesota banks responded favorably to a request that service charges and transaction fees on these trust accounts be waived. The Committee recommends that the MSBA and the LTAB work together to encourage Minnesota banks to restore the interest rates on lawyers' trust accounts. Even a one percent increase would substantially increase the revenue available to LTAB for distribution to legal services programs. With IOLTA income averaging just under $1 million a year, a one percent increase would generate another $1 million a year.

F. **Attorney Registration Fee Increase. To ensure that all lawyers assume an increased part of the responsibility for funding legal service providers, beyond the voluntary financial contributions that many individual lawyers already make, the Supreme Court should be petitioned to increase the annual lawyer registration fee by $50 for lawyers practicing more than three years, and $25 for lawyers practicing three years or less, with the increase going to the Legal Services Advisory Committee for allocation to legal services providers, including volunteer attorney programs.**

Although the Committee believes that lawyers are not solely responsible for meeting the unmet need for civil legal services, lawyers are the gatekeepers of justice, and should take the lead. Lawyers in effect have a monopoly, as only they can provide legal advice and represent parties before the courts. Lawyers in Minnesota are already donating over $3.5 million in legal services each year through the Coalition programs alone, with considerably more legal services donated directly and through other organized programs. Lawyers are also already making financial contributions of over $500,000 each year directly to legal services providers. While these contributions are impressive, the Committee believes that all lawyers should assume an increased part of the responsibility for funding legal services.

The Committee recommends that the Supreme Court adopt in 1996 an increase in lawyers' annual registration fees of $25 for all lawyers not otherwise exempt, and $50 for lawyers admitted over three years. The funds could be distributed through the Court's Legal Services Advisory Committee pursuant to Minn. Stat. §§ 480.24 et seq., which provide that at least 85 percent of the funds go proportionately to the six programs which together serve the entire state, and the

---

[18] IOLTA rates were 5.25 percent in 1987, and 1.01 percent on December 31, 1995. The prime rates were 8.1 percent in 1987, and 8.75 percent on December 31, 1995.

balance of up to 15 percent be distributed through grants to programs serving eligible clients, including the volunteer attorney programs.

The Committee believes that **all** lawyers, not just those already volunteering time and/or contributing money, have an obligation to help ensure that all Minnesotans have meaningful access to justice. There are over 20,000 registered lawyers in Minnesota. Of these, over 17,000 are practicing, 2,452 are nonresidents, 755 are retired, and 100 are in the armed forces. The current registration fee is $142; those admitted less than three years pay $42.

In discussing the amount of the increase in registration fees, the Committee initially considered a $100 increase. After learning of the Lawyers Professional Responsibility Board plans to petition the Court for an increase of $20 per year to support its operations, and of other possible fee increases, the Committee scaled back its recommended increase. The Committee's recommendation of an increase in attorney registration fees of $50 for lawyers practicing more than three years, and $25 for those practicing for three years or less is the equivalent of only half an hour of most lawyers' billable time. This amount, a dollar a week, does not seem unreasonable. The Committee notes that it represents one percent of the aspirational standard set forth in revised Rule 6.1 of the Rules of Professional Conduct, recently adopted by the Supreme Court.

The Committee discussed the petition filed with the Supreme Court by the MSBA in 1982 for a one-time $25 increase in the attorney registration fee, also to support civil legal services. That petition was denied by the Court without an opinion. Arguments were presented to the Court at that time with respect to the constitutionality of such a fee. The Committee recognizes that the outcome of a petition for a fee increase is uncertain. However, the Committee believes that ensuring access to justice for the poor is an integral part of the role of lawyers and judges in the judicial system. It is as essential to the integrity of the profession and the healthy functioning of the judicial branch of government as continuing education of lawyers, eliminating discrimination within the bench and bar, creating a client security fund to protect clients against theft by their lawyers, and enforcement of the disciplinary rules, all of which have been adopted by the Court, and carry mandatory direct or indirect costs for lawyers. In 1987, the Supreme Court created the Client Security Fund assessment in the face of constitutional objections similar to those raised in 1982. The Committee believes that the Supreme Court, within its constitutional responsibility to oversee the judicial branch of government, has the power to take steps to ensure that all citizens have access to that branch of government, including steps which impose a cost on lawyers, who enjoy a legal monopoly as gatekeepers to the justicial system.

The Committee does not expect to file a petition with the Supreme Court to request this increase until summer of 1996. The Committee believes that it is important for the Minnesota State Bar Association to have an opportunity to consider this report and the Committee's recommendations. While the Committee strongly supports this recommendation, the Committee recognizes that concerns exist about such a fee increase, including its possible impact on bar association memberships and on efforts to increase donations of time and money by lawyers. However, many Committee members received significant positive feedback at the local level in informal discussions before the Committee voted in favor of this recommendation. The Committee believes that widespread discussion of the proposal at the local level, including consideration of the critical and growing unmet need for legal assistance, will generate support for the recommendation.

G. Conclusion.

Lawyers have a special responsibility to help ensure that all people have access to our system of justice. Many have demonstrated, with both time and money, that they are willing to do their part. More needs to be done, and **all** lawyers need to be involved. However, the entire burden cannot and should not fall on their shoulders. By way of comparison, private doctors are not expected to meet all the medical needs of the poor without pay. Access to justice is fundamental to our system of government, and all Americans have a stake in securing respect for the law. This cannot happen unless the system is both just and accessible to all citizens, rich or poor.

SECTION 2

SECTION 2: ADOPTION OF RULES AND POLICIES THAT PROMOTE PRO BONO PARTICIPATION

Modification of Pro Bono Ethical Rule

Discussion

Almost every state has an ethical rule that calls upon lawyers to render pro bono service. For those states in which the Rules of Professional Conduct are in effect, the pro bono responsibility is defined in Rule 6.1; for states operating under the older Code of Professional Responsibility, the pro bono obligation is explained in EC 2-25. Since 1990, nine states have amended their pro bono rule to add specificity to the definition of pro bono work and/or to emphasize the provision of pro bono service to persons of limited means.

In 1993, the ABA House of Delegates adopted revisions to Model Rule of Professional Conduct 6.1. One of the objectives of revised Model Rule 6.1 was to provide specific guidance to lawyers regarding the amount of pro bono service they should aspire to render annually. Another goal was to provide a viable response to the increasing need for pro bono attorney involvement in the delivery of legal services to the poor. The rule's emphasis on service to persons of limited means represents a recognition of the seriousness of the problem, and demonstrates the ABA's belief that bar members must play an active role in solving it.

Similarly, state and local bar associations' support for adoption of revisions to their state's pro bono ethical rule in a manner similar to revised Model Rule 6.1 demonstrates their commitment to increasing the private bar's role in delivering legal services to the poor. In addition, adoption of such revisions provides specific guidance to lawyers and law students who turn to the state's ethical rules to determine the standard of conduct that is expected of them in rendering pro bono service.

While it is ultimately the responsibility of another entity (usually a state's supreme court) to adopt revisions to state ethical rules, bar associations can take a leadership role by filing a petition with the court or taking other appropriate steps to initiate amendment of the pro bono ethical rule.

The following state supreme courts have either adopted revised Model Rule 6.1, or otherwise revised their ethical rule to specify the amount of recommended pro bono service and/or add an emphasis on service to the poor:

Adopted Revised Model Rule 6.1	Otherwise Revised the Pro Bono Ethical Rule
Hawaii	Arizona
Montana	Kentucky
Minnesota	Georgia
	Florida
	Virginia
	Nevada

The adoption of revised Model Rule 6.1 is currently under consideration by the Mississippi Supreme Court.

Pros

☞ Bar support for the adoption of revised Model Rule 6.1 or similar revisions to the pro bono ethical rule demonstrates the bar's recognition of the problem of access to the legal system, and the bar's commitment to address it.

☞ Although the rule's language is aspirational and not mandatory in nature, a bar association's support for the adoption of revised Model Rule 6.1 or similar revisions to the pro bono ethical rule demonstrates the association's formal encouragement of its members to perform pro bono services.

☞ The adoption of revised Model Rule 6.1 or similar revisions to the pro bono ethical rule provides attorneys with guidance on the delivery of pro bono services, both in terms of how many hours are encouraged and what types of legal services constitute pro bono.

☞ A bar association's consideration of revised Model Rule 6.1 or similar revisions to the pro bono ethical rule generates a dialogue that is healthy for the association.

Cons

☞ Attorneys may interpret adoption of revised Model Rule 6.1 or similar revisions to the pro bono ethical rule as evidence of a future intent to adopt a mandatory rule.

☞ The process of obtaining support for and adoption of a revised rule can be time-consuming and require the expenditure of substantial volunteer resources.

Contacts

Minnesota State Bar Association
Staff Contact: Nancy Kleeman, Director, Volunteer Legal Services (612) 673-6331
Volunteer Contact: James L. Baillie (612) 347-7013

Montana Bar Association
Staff Contact: Judy Williams, State Pro Bono Support Director (406) 252-6351
Volunteer Contacts: Honorable Karla M. Gray (406) 444-2621
Harley Harris (406) 444-2026

State Bar of Georgia
Staff Contact: Ayres Gardner, State Pro Bono Support Director (404) 527-8762
Volunteer Contact: Benjamin F. Easterlin, IV (912) 924-9316

Examples

Revised Model Rule 6.1, ABA Model Rules of Professional Conduct (Attachment 2-A)

Amended Rule 3-102, EC 2-25, Rules and Regulations of the State Bar of Georgia (Attachment 2-B)

Adoption of Resolutions and Policies that Encourage Pro Bono Participation

Discussion

The adoption of resolutions that encourage pro bono participation is a relatively simple way in which bar associations can demonstrate their recognition of the bar's responsibility to participate in the delivery of legal services to persons of limited means. Bar resolutions take many forms. Some are very general in nature, simply noting that there is a crisis in the delivery of legal services to persons of limited means, and encouraging bar members to assist in solving the problem. Other resolutions include specific recommendations regarding how bar members can contribute pro bono services, including number of hours and type of work. Bar resolutions also can serve to promote cooperative pro bono efforts between the bar and other entities, such as the judiciary.

For bar associations that do not have a history of institutional pro bono involvement, resolutions are an effective initial step in developing a pro bono culture. Pro bono resolutions generally are not threatening to the membership, and therefore, are relatively easy to pass. They form a basis upon which a pro bono culture gradually can be built through the education of bar members about the significant unmet legal needs of persons of limited means.

In 1995, the American Bar Association House of Delegates adopted a resolution urging bar associations to make the expansion of pro bono legal services a critical priority. The resolution also urges bar associations to develop effective and innovative strategies for promoting pro bono activities. The governing bodies of a number of state bar associations have passed resolutions encouraging their members to perform pro bono services and/or contribute financially to pro bono or legal services programs. Many local bars have passed similar resolutions. In addition, practice sections within state and local bars have passed resolutions encouraging pro bono services.

In addition to the passage of resolutions, bar associations should consider the adoption of specific policies relating to pro bono. Such policies include, but are not limited to, those that encourage: bar officers and committee chairs to perform pro bono service; bar sections to form pro bono committees and implement pro bono projects; and law firms, corporate law departments, governmental agencies and area law schools to promote/require pro bono services.
In a number of states, for example, model policies have been adopted promoting pro bono participation by specific groups of attorneys, including staff attorneys in Attorney General offices and corporate counsel attorneys.

Pros

☞ Pro bono resolutions and policies demonstrate the bar's commitment to pro bono services.

☞ Resolutions require minimal administrative time and expense.

☞ Pro bono resolutions generally are easy to pass.

Cons

☞ Resolutions are easily forgotten and have minimal impact, unless specific action results from them.

☞ Too much debate over the definition of pro bono can divert attention from doing necessary work and divide a formerly unified team.

Contacts

Minnesota State Bar Association
Staff Contact: Nancy Kleeman, Director,Volunteer Legal Services (612) 673-6331
Volunteer Contact: James L. Baillie (612) 347-7013

The State Bar of California
Staff Contact: Mary Viviano, Director, Office of Legal Services (415) 561-8250
Volunteer Contact: Jack Londen (415) 677-7415

New Hampshire Bar Association
Staff Contact: Jeannine McCoy, Executive Director (603) 224-6942
Volunteer Contact: L. Jonathan Ross (603) 669-2211

Harrisonburg/Rockingham Bar Association (Virginia)
Staff Contact: John Whitfield, Executive Director (703) 433-1830
Volunteer Contact: Gregory St. Ours (703) 434-0316

Chicago Bar Association
Staff Contact: Linda Rio, Chicago Bar Foundation (312) 554-1204
Volunteer Contact: Bob Glaves (312) 553-8633

Examples

1995 American Bar Association Resolution Urging Bar Associations to Develop Strategies to Promote Pro Bono Services (Attachment 2-C)

The State Bar of California Resolution Requesting Cooperation of Judicial Council to Increase Pro Bono Efforts and Judicial Council Resolution (Attachment 2-D)

State of Minnesota Office of the Attorney General Pro Bono Policy (Attachment 2-E)

Chicago Bar Association Resolution Regarding Pro Bono Legal Services (Attachment 2-F)

Adoption of Mandatory or Voluntary Reporting Requirement

Discussion

Several state bar associations or state supreme courts have considered the adoption of a requirement that attorneys report their pro bono activity. Reporting requirements generally have arisen out of studies and reports done by bar committees or special commissions appointed by the court. These studies and reports typically assess the unmet legal needs of persons of limited means, and recommend options for addressing them. In some situations, mandatory pro bono service has been considered along with some form of a reporting requirement. In considering either option, the entities making the recommendation generally have relied on the ethical principle that pro bono legal service to the poor is an integral part of a lawyer's public service responsibility.

As of June 1, 1996, Florida is the only state to adopt a mandatory reporting requirement. In 1993, the Florida Supreme Court began requiring attorneys to report annually whether they have performed twenty hours of direct pro bono legal services or contributed $350 or more to a legal services organization. Subsequent opinions clarified the reporting requirement. Reporting is done on attorneys' annual Florida Bar dues statements. Pro bono legal services providers in Florida indicate that participation in organized programs has risen sharply since the reporting requirement went into effect. In addition, many attorneys continue to perform pro bono services in their own practices, outside of organized pro bono programs.

Texas, Kentucky, New Mexico, Maryland and Hawaii have voluntary pro bono reporting systems in place. In Texas, the reporting requirement was instituted by the state bar. The system originated in the Texas legislature, which in its sunset review of the bar adopted the State Bar Act, directing the bar to analyze whether mandatory pro bono should be implemented in the state. The state bar board ultimately adopted a recommendation for a voluntary reporting system. In Texas, Kentucky and New Mexico, the pro bono reporting form is a part of the annual bar dues statement. In Maryland, voluntary reporting is done on a survey distributed by the Clients' Security Trust Fund. The survey is prepared by People's Pro Bono Action Center, Inc., a statewide pro bono support program, and is mailed to all Maryland attorneys by the Chief Judge of the Court of Appeals of Maryland. In Hawaii, the Hawaii State Bar Association recently approved an optional question on the Attorney Registration Statement regarding the number of pro bono hours provided by bar members during the past 12 months. The Chicago Bar Association also has instituted a voluntary reporting requirement.

Pros

- ☞ Reporting may lead to increased pro bono activity by members of the bar.
- ☞ Reporting provides a mechanism for tracking the level of pro bono activity.

Cons

- ☞ Reporting requirements may appear to pose the threat of a future intent to invoke mandatory pro bono service.
- ☞ Reporting requirements are administratively intensive.

Contacts

Florida Voluntary Attorney Pro Bono Plan
Staff Contact: Kent Spuhler, Director, Florida Legal Services, Inc. (904) 385-7900
Volunteer Contact: Honorable William Van Nortwick, Jr., First District Court of Appeal (904) 488-6151

Texas Lawyers Care
Staff Contact: Julie Oliver, Executive Director (512) 463-1463 x 2155
Volunteer Contact: Kirk Watson (512) 476-4346

Kentucky Bar Association
Staff Contact: Bruce Davis, Executive Director, (502) 564-3795

New Mexico Bar Association
Staff Contact: Rufina Hernandez, Executive Director (505) 842-6132
Volunteer Contact: Sara Singleton, State Bar President (505) 243-2615

People's Pro Bono Action Center, Inc. (Maryland)
Staff Contact: Sharon Goldsmith, Executive Director (410) 837-9379
Volunteer Contact: Lee A. Caplin (301) 759-1000

Hawaii State Bar Association
Staff Contact: Coralle Chun Matayoshi, Executive Director (808) 537-1868
Volunteer Contact: Ellen Godbey Carson (808) 524-1800

Chicago Bar Association
Staff Contact: Linda Rio, Chicago Bar Foundation (312) 554-1204
Volunteer Contact: Bob Glaves (312) 553-8633

Examples

Florida Bar Dues Statement Reporting Form (Attachment 2-G)

Texas Bar Dues Statement Voluntary Reporting Form (Attachment 2-H)

Chicago Bar Association Resolution and Voluntary Pro Bono Activity Report (Attachment 2-I)

Adoption of Rule Requiring Pro Bono Participation by Members

Discussion

There are no state bar associations requiring mandatory pro bono service as a condition of membership. Several local voluntary bar associations require mandatory pro bono service or a financial contribution as a condition of membership. The Orange County Bar Association in Orlando, Florida requires that members either handle two pro bono cases a year or donate at least $350.00 to the Legal Aid Society of the bar association. Similar requirements have been adopted by the Mercer County Bar Association (Pennsylvania), the El Paso Bar Association (Texas), and the DuPage County Bar Association (Illinois).

Pros

- ☞ Mandatory pro bono service may increase the level of pro bono participation by attorneys.
- ☞ Mandatory pro bono service enables the bar association to track pro bono activity of its members.
- ☞ Mandatory pro bono service demonstrates the bar's commitment to pro bono activity.

Cons

- ☞ Mandatory pro bono service requirements may invoke strong negative reactions from some bar members.
- ☞ Tracking and enforcement of required pro bono service is administratively intensive.

Contacts

Legal Aid Society of Orange County Bar Association (Florida)
Staff Contact: Catherine Tucker, Executive Director (407) 841-8310
Volunteer Contact: Lawrence Matthews (407) 872-2200

Mercer County Bar Association (Pennsylvania)
Staff Contact: Carl Moses, Executive Director (412) 346-6112

DuPage County Bar Association (Illinois)
Staff Contact: Brenda Carroll (603) 653-6212
Volunteer Contact: John Barsanti (603) 980-6973

SECTION 2 ATTACHMENTS

MODEL RULES OF PROFESSIONAL CONDUCT

RULE 6.1 VOLUNTARY PRO BONO PUBLICO SERVICE

A lawyer should aspire to render at least (50) hours of pro bono publico legal services per year. In fulfilling this responsibility, the lawyer should:

(a) provide a substantial majority of the (50) hours of legal services without fee or expectation of fee to:
(1) persons of limited means or
(2) charitable, religious, civic, community, governmental and educational organizations in matters which are designed primarily to address the needs of persons of limited means; and

(b) provide any additional services through:
(1) delivery of legal services at no fee or substantially reduced fee to individuals, groups or organizations seeking to secure or protect civil rights, civil liberties or public rights, or charitable, religious, civic, community, governmental and educational organizations in matters in furtherance of their organizational purposes, where the payment of standard legal fees would significantly deplete the organization's economic resources or would be otherwise inappropriate;
(2) delivery of legal services at a substantially reduced fee to persons of limited means; or
(3) participation in activities for improving the law, the legal system or the legal profession.

In addition, a lawyer should voluntarily contribute financial support to organizations that provide legal services to persons of limited means.

Comment

Every lawyer, regardless of professional prominence or professional work load, has a responsibility to provide legal services to those unable to pay, and personal involvement in the problems of the disadvantaged can be one of the most rewarding experiences in the life of a lawyer. The American Bar Association urges all lawyers to provide a minimum of 50 hours of pro bono services annually. States, however, may decide to choose a higher or lower number of hours of annual service (which may be expressed as a percentage of a lawyer's professional time) depending upon local needs and local conditions. It is recognized that in some years a lawyer may render greater or fewer hours than the annual standard specified, but during the course of his or her legal career, each lawyer should render on average per year, the number of hours set forth in this Rule. Services can be performed in civil matters or in criminal or quasi-criminal matters for which there is no government obligation to provide funds for legal representation, such as post-conviction death penalty appeal cases.

Paragraphs (a)(1) and (2) recognize the critical need for legal services that exists among persons of limited means by providing that a substantial majority of the legal services rendered annually to the disadvantaged be furnished without fee or expectation of fee. Legal services under these paragraphs consist of a full range of activities, including individual and class representation, the provision of legal advice, legislative lobbying, administrative rule making and the provision of free training or mentoring to those who represent persons of limited means. The variety of these activities should facilitate participation by government attorneys, even when restrictions exist on their engaging in the outside practice of law.

Persons eligible for legal services under paragraphs (a)(1) and (2) are those who qualify for participation in programs funded by the Legal Services Corporation and those whose incomes and financial resources are slightly above the guidelines utilized by such programs but nevertheless, cannot afford counsel. Legal services can be rendered to individuals or to organizations such as homeless shelters, battered women's centers and food pantries that serve those of limited means. The term "governmental organizations" includes, but is not limited to, public protection programs and sections of governmental or public sector agencies.

Because service must be provided without fee or expectation of fee, the intent of the lawyer to render free legal services is essential for the work performed to fall within the meaning of paragraphs (a)(1) and (2). Accordingly, services rendered cannot be considered pro bono if an anticipated fee is uncollected, but the award of statutory attorneys' fees in a case originally accepted as pro bono would not disqualify such services from inclusion under this section. Lawyers who do receive fees in such cases are encouraged to contribute an appropriate portion of such fees to organizations or projects that benefit persons of limited means.

While it is possible for a lawyer to fulfill the annual responsibility to perform pro bono services exclusively through activities described in paragraphs (a)(1) and (2), to the extent that any hours of service remained unfulfilled, the remaining commitment can be met in a variety of ways as set forth in paragraph (b). Constitutional, statutory or regulatory restrictions may prohibit or impede government and public sector lawyers and judges from performing the pro bono services outlined in paragraphs (a)(1) and (2). Accordingly, where those restrictions apply, government and public sector lawyers and judges may fulfill their pro bono responsibility by performing services outlined in paragraph (b).

Paragraph (b)(1) includes the provision of certain types of legal services to those whose incomes and financial resources place them above limited means. It also permits the pro bono attorney to accept a substantially reduced fee for services. Examples of the types of issues that may be addressed under this paragraph include First Amendment claims, Title VII claims and environmental protection claims. Additionally, a wide range of organizations may be represented, including social service, medical research, cultural and religious groups.

Paragraph (b)(2) covers instances in which attorneys agree to and receive a modest fee for furnishing legal services to persons of limited means. Participation in judicare programs and acceptance of court appointments in which the fee is substantially below a lawyer's usual rate are encouraged under this section.

Paragraph (b)(3) recognizes the value of lawyers engaging in activities that improve the law, the legal system or the legal profession. Serving on bar association committees, serving on boards of pro bono or legal services programs, taking part in Law Day activities, acting as a continuing legal education instructor, a mediator or an arbitrator and engaging in legislative lobbying to improve the law, the legal system or the profession are a few examples of the many activities that fall within this paragraph.

Because the provision of pro bono services is a professional responsibility, it is the individual ethical commitment of each lawyer. Nevertheless, there may be times when it is not feasible for a lawyer to engage in pro bono services. At such times a lawyer may discharge the pro bono responsibility by providing financial support to organizations providing free legal services to persons of limited means. Such financial support should be reasonably equivalent to the value of the hours of service that would have otherwise been provided. In addition, at times it may be more feasible to satisfy the pro bono responsibility collectively, as by a firm's aggregate pro bono activities.

Because the efforts of individual lawyers are not enough to meet the need for free legal services that exists among persons of limited means, the government and the profession have instituted additional programs to provide those services. Every lawyer should financially support such programs, in addition to either providing direct pro bono services or making financial contributions when pro bono service is not feasible.

The responsibility set forth in this Rule is not intended to be enforced through disciplinary process.

SUPREME COURT OF GEORGIA

ATLANTA FEB 1 1 1993

The Honorable Supreme Court met pursuant to adjournment.

The following order was passed:

The Court having considered the motion to amend the Rules and Regulations of the State Bar of Georgia filed on July 16, 1992, it is ordered that the Rules and Regulations for the Organization and Government of the State Bar of Georgia be amended as follows:

Rule 7-102, Rule 3-102, EC 2-25, and Rule 4-204.3 are hereby amended to read as follows, and said rules and regulations are further amended by the addition of EC 1-7, EC 1-8, and EC 1-9 to Rule 3-101 and the addition of Standard 71 and Standard 72 to Rule 4-102 to read as follows:

(See Exhibit 1 attached hereto)

Those proposed amendments contained in the motion of July 16, 1992 which are not specifically addressed in this order will be considered by the Court within ninety days.

SUPREME COURT OF THE STATE OF GEORGIA,

CLERK'S OFFICE, ATLANTA

I certify that the above is a true extract from the minutes of the Supreme Court of Georgia.

Witness my signature and the seal of said court hereto affixed the day and year last above written.

Sherie M. Welch, Clerk

Rule 3-102, EC 2-25.

EC-2-25

(a) Historically, the need for legal services of those unable to pay reasonable fees has been met in part by lawyers who donated their services or accepted court appointments on behalf of such individuals. The basic responsibility for providing legal services for those unable to pay ultimately rests upon the individual lawyer, and personal involvement in the problems of the disadvantaged can be one of the most rewarding experiences in the life of a lawyer. Every lawyer, regardless of professional prominence or professional workload, should find time to participate in serving the disadvantaged. The rendition of free legal services to those unable to pay reasonable fees continues to be an obligation of each lawyer, but the efforts of individual lawyers are often not enough to meet the need. Thus it has been necessary for the profession to institute additional programs to provide legal services. Accordingly, legal aid offices, lawyer referral services, and other related programs have been developed, and others will be developed, by the profession. Every lawyer should support all proper efforts to meet this need for legal services.

(b) "Pro Bono Publico", or "Pro Bono", service includes all uncompensated services performed by attorneys for the public good. Such service includes civic, charitable, and public service activities, as well as activities that improve the law, the legal system, and the legal profession. The direct provision of legal services to the poor, without an expectation of compensation, is the most important and needed type of pro bono service. Direct provision of legal services to the poor includes representation in civil matters and representation in criminal cases.

(c) Although the amount of time which each attorney devotes to pro bono service is a matter of individual conscience, the following are suggested guidelines: each attorney in Georgia should endeavor to perform 40 hours annually, or 120 hours over a three year period, of such service. Of this total, the attorney should endeavor to devote 20 hours annually, or 60 hours over a three year period, to work involving the direct provision of legal services to the poor, without an expectation of compensation.

Adopted by the ABA House of Delegates on August 9, 1995

AMERICAN BAR ASSOCIATION

STANDING COMMITTEE ON LAWYERS' PUBLIC SERVICE RESPONSIBILITY
SECTION OF LITIGATION
CONSORTIUM ON LEGAL SERVICES AND THE PUBLIC
YOUNG LAWYERS DIVISION
SECTION OF INDIVIDUAL RIGHTS AND RESPONSIBILITIES
STANDING COMMITTEE ON LEGAL ASSISTANTS
STANDING COMMITTEE ON LAWYER REFERRAL AND INFORMATION
COMMISSION ON DOMESTIC VIOLENCE
HAWAII STATE BAR ASSOCIATION
STATE BAR OF MONTANA
HENNEPIN COUNTY BAR ASSOCIATION
NASHVILLE BAR ASSOCIATION
PHILADELPHIA BAR ASSOCIATION
MONROE COUNTY BAR ASSOCIATION

RECOMMENDATION

RESOLVED, that the American Bar Association, along with other national, state territorial and local bar associations are strongly urged to make the expansion of *pro bono* legal services by practicing lawyers a critical priority for the bar.

FURTHER RESOLVED, that these bar associations are encouraged to develop effective and innovative strategies to promote pro bono service and to allocate sufficient bar resources to ensure that these strategies can be effectively implemented.

FURTHER RESOLVED, that in developing these strategies, bar associations should coordinate with legal services providers and *pro bono* programs.

FURTHER RESOLVED, that in developing these strategies, bar associations should consider including the following activities:

1. Advocating for the adoption of Model Rule of Professional Conduct 6.1 (Voluntary Pro Bono Publico Service) (revised 1993) as part of state ethics rules;

2. Adopting a voluntary or mandatory mechanism for bar members to annually report the type of *pro bono* service performed, the number of *pro bono* hours rendered and any financial contributions made to legal services and *pro bono* organizations;

3. Encouraging candidates for bar leadership positions to demonstrate their record of support for *pro bono* and legal services through *pro bono* service, service on the board of a *pro bono* or legal services organization or other relevant activities;

4. Encouraging and assisting large law firms, corporate law departments, government agencies and law schools to adopt policies that promote and facilitate *pro bono* participation; and

5. Creating or enhancing a standing bar committee on *pro bono* service that, in cooperation with bar officers and with the assistance of bar staff develops a comprehensive long-range plan for increasing the availability of *pro bono* and other free legal services, and ensures that legal services and *pro bono* issues are identified as critical bar priorities.

THE STATE BAR OF CALIFORNIA

RESOLUTION ADOPTED BY THE BOARD OF GOVERNORS
OCTOBER 28, 1995

RESOLVED, upon recommendation of the Board Committees on Legal Services, and Courts and Legislation, that the Board hereby requests the Judicial Council to join with the State Bar and others in a cooperative effort to address the impending crisis in legal services that will result if federal funding cuts and restrictions proposed for the Legal Services Corporation are enacted, including representation in newly restricted pending cases handled by legal services attorneys, an increased number of pro per litigants in the courts and a need for expanded pro bono activities.

I hereby certify that the foregoing is a full, true and correct copy of a resolution adopted by the Board of Governors at its meeting held on October 28, 1995, in Oakland, California.

Jeffrey T. Gersick
Secretary

Date: June 12, 1996

JUDICIAL COUNCIL RESOLUTION

Unanimously Endorsed by the Judicial Council of California
May 17, 1996

RESOLVED, that the Judicial Council of California will join the State Bar of California to launch a cooperative effort to broaden access to the courts for unrepresented and low- or middle-income persons; this access is threatened due to the lack of adequate funding for legal services programs serving the poor. There presently are an increasing number of litigants who must represent themselves without the assistance of counsel, and the lack of funding for legal services programs further diminishes access to our judicial system for those without adequate financial resources.

The Judicial Council urges members of the California judiciary to help address this urgent need by contributing to the effort to encourage pro bono legal work; such as:

(1) agreeing to sign pro bono recruitment letters on behalf of pro bono programs;

(2) participating in pro bono recognition events;

(3) assisting in the training of pro bono lawyers;

(4) considering special accommodation for counsel who are volunteering their services on behalf of the indigent, such as allowing pro bono attorneys to be heard first on the calendar, setting pro bono cases at specific times, or allowing pro bono attorneys to attend routine hearings by conference call; and

(5) working closely with pro bono programs to make clinics available at or near the courthouse for those who cannot otherwise afford counsel.

STATE OF MINNESOTA

Office of the Attorney General

PRO BONO POLICY

I. POLICY.

This office is committed to legal service in the public interest. It seeks to hire and retain staff members who share that commitment. The office recognizes that, in addition to the significant public interest work performed by staff as part of their employment with the state, individual staff members may also desire to provide legal assistance to the disadvantaged without charge. It is the policy of this office to allow and support such activity.

There is a serious unmet need for legal services for persons of limited means as documented in numerous studies in Minnesota and across the nation. The shortage in such services prompted the Minnesota State Bar Association several years ago to adopt an aspirational standard which encourages attorneys to provide pro bono legal services of 50 hours per year with at least 25 hours devoted to direct legal services to low income persons. The American Bar Association has adopted a similar standard. Given the unmet need and the Minnesota State Bar Association's aspirational standard, the office has determined that the provision of pro bono services, including a limited use of state resources as outlined below, is consistent with and furthers the state's interests. Each attorney must make his or her own decision about participation in pro bono activities, depending on other professional and personal commitments. Nevertheless, the Office encourages each staff member to consider ways to engage in pro bono activities.

II. PRO BONO SERVICES.

A. Pro bono services include both the pro bono representation of clients and non-litigation volunteer activities. As used in this policy, "pro bono services" means:

1. Providing legal services without remuneration to:

a. Persons of limited means; or

b. Charitable, religious, civic, community, governmental and educational organizations in matters which are designed primarily to address the needs of persons of limited means; and

2. Providing additional law related services without remuneration through:

a. The delivery of legal services to individuals, groups or organizations seeking to secure or protect civil rights, civil liberties or public rights, or charitable, religious, civic, community, governmental and educational organizations in matters in furtherance of their organizational purposes, where the payment of standard legal fees would significantly deplete the organization's economic resources or would otherwise be inappropriate; or

b. Participation in activities for improving the law, the legal system or the legal profession.[1]

B. Examples of pro bono activities which may be approved include, but are not limited to:

1. Representation of individual clients;

2. Serving as a guardian ad litem;

3. Providing representation to nonprofit organizations;

4. Providing advice as part of a Legal Services Corporation program:

a. In landlord/tenant or consumer matters;

b. On wills, powers of attorney, and private guardianship;

5. Performing research for or rendering expert advice to providers of legal services to the low income and disadvantaged;

6. Participating on the board of a legal services organization;

7. Providing training or preparing materials for seminars or other educational activities involving poverty law issues;

8. Participating on Bar committees and projects relating to the delivery of legal services and pro bono legal services.

---

1. This policy is not intended to affect any other policies of the Attorney General's Office regarding participation in Bar activities.

III. PROCEDURES.

A. Approval.

Participation in pro bono activities must be approved in advance by the Division Manager. In order to identify pro bono opportunities generally available to staff, the Pro Bono Committee will review major referring programs identified by staff or others, and upon approval by the Chief Deputy, will notify staff of programs which meet office criteria.

The following criteria will be used by the division manager when approving a staff member's participation in a particular activity, and by the Pro Bono Committee when reviewing programs for general approval:

1. Whether the request is consistent with the terms and purpose of this policy.

2. Whether a conflict of interest exists under the Rules of Professional Responsibility.[2]

3. Whether malpractice coverage exists.

4. Whether the high profile or controversial nature of the subject matter may lead to an unacceptable public perception that the Attorney General's Office is participating in the activity. Participation in a pro bono activity opposing a State agency is discouraged and must be approved by the Chief Deputy.

5. Whether the amount of time necessary to perform the activity would adversely affect the staff member's ability to discharge his or her office responsibilities.

6. Whether the case would require establishment of a trust account by the staff member. Staff will not be permitted to handle such cases. Trust accounts, where necessary, must be established and maintained by referring programs.

7. In matters involving legal representation of a nonprofit organization, whether the representation may involve issues subject to regulation by the Attorney General pursuant to chapters 309, 317A and 501B of Minnesota Statutes. Staff should not provide legal representation

---

2. The *Comments of the Office of the Attorney General on the Minnesota Rules of Professional Conduct* should be consulted in determining whether a conflict of interest exists.

concerning such issues as governance disputes, formation or dissolution of an organization, IRS matters, accounting practices, charitable solicitations, conflicts of interest or the use or proposed use of assets held for charitable purposes. To the extent that staff members who are directors of nonprofit organizations become involved in such issues, they should clarify they are doing so as directors of the organization, not as lawyers for the organization.[3]

B. Staff members should obtain approval from the Division Manager for each new pro bono client, should continue to comply with these criteria, and should consult with the Division Manager or Committee if he or she has questions.

C. Continuing participation.

If, after approval for a pro bono project, the circumstances related to the representation change in a manner that significantly impact one or more of the factors referenced in Section III.A. above, the staff member must consult with the Division Manager to discuss the change in circumstances and continued participation of the staff member in the activity.

Similarly, the staff member's manager must be contacted if it appears that the matter will be more time consuming or complex than originally contemplated.

D. Representation of pro bono clients.

1. The potential client must be informed that a conflicts check must be made before acceptance of the case. No discussion with the prospective client should take place if it is immediately apparent that a conflict exists. After the first meeting with the client, the staff member is responsible for determining whether any potential conflicts exist. The Pro Bono Committee shall develop a check list to assist in this determination. The division manager must maintain a list of pro bono activities in which division members are engaged in order to assist with the evaluation of possible conflicts.

---

3. The office policy permits staff members to serve as directors of nonprofit organizations. However, staff members who become directors of nonprofits must notify the Chief Deputy and the manager of the Charities Division.

2. Before agreeing to accept a pro bono client the attorney should determine whether the referring program or organization has a malpractice insurance policy which covers volunteer attorneys. This office does not provide malpractice coverage for pro bono work. A staff member's pro bono work is not within the scope of his or her employment with the State; the State does not assume any liability for this work.

3. Accepting a pro bono case.

   a. Following approval of pro bono activity, a retainer letter, specifically confirming the scope of the representation, and outlining the client's obligations and responsibilities, should be sent to the client. (The Pro Bono Committee will make available a model letter.) A copy must be maintained in the attorney's file. The staff member is responsible for making it clear to the client, any opposing parties, or others involved in a pro bono case or activity, that the staff member is acting in his or her individual capacity as a volunteer, and is not acting as a representative of, or on behalf of the office.

   b. The client should be informed how, when, and where to contact the attorney by telephone or letter.

4. Case file responsibility.

   An attorney participating in a pro bono project or matter is personally responsible for his or her pro bono files.

IV. IDENTIFICATION WITH THE OFFICE.

Staff members who participate in pro bono activities or in providing pro bono services may not indicate or represent in any way that they are acting on behalf of the office or in their official capacity. If a staff member has any reason to believe that those receiving service, opposing counsel, or the courts mistakenly believe that a staff member is acting in an official role, staff must make a clear disclaimer that they are not acting on behalf of the officer or in their official capacity. For example, if a staff member is known to opposing counsel or the court as a member of the Attorney General's staff, a disclaimer must be made.

A. The staff member may not use office business cards or otherwise identify himself or herself as a government attorney in any communication, correspondence or pleading connected with pro bono activities. It is PREFErred that correspondence be handled through the coordinating legal services organization or received at the staff member's home address. However, if this would present an undue hardship, the office address may be used if the address does not include the office name or indicate the nature of the office.

B. The general office telephone number may not be used for pro bono activities. Phone calls may be received either on the staff member's individual line, through the referring program or organization, or at the staff member's home.

C. The office may not be used for meetings with clients or opposing counsel in a pro bono case.

V. USE OF OFFICE RESOURCES.

A. Hours of work.

When performance of pro bono work is required during regular work hours, the staff member may request that his or her manager approve a flexible work schedule, in accordance with section III of the Office Manual, to accommodate the time needed for pro bono work or vacation leave may be used. In unusual circumstances, and with prior approval, the staff member may take leave without pay.

B. Telephone calls.

Local telephone calls may be made from the staff member's individual line. Long distance telephone calls may not be charged to the office.

C. Offices/Library.

Staff members may use their individual offices to do research and to draft pleadings, briefs, letters or other written materials. The library may also be used for doing research related to pro bono projects. Such work must be done in a manner which does not interfere with the performance of the office's or staff member's regular functions or duties and responsibilities. Office computer research facilities (e.g., Lexis or Westlaw) may not be used to do pro bono research.

D. Clerical support.

Clerical services should be obtained from the coordinating agency when available. This office will explore the possibility of making clerical support available, consistent with state law and union work rules.

E. Supplies and equipment.

1. Staff members may use word processing and dictation equipment so long as such use does not interfere with the performance of the office's or the staff member's regular functions or duties and responsibilities.

2. A limited amount of office supplies (not including stamps), photocopying, and non-long distance fax use is available to staff members performing pro bono work consistent with other provisions of this policy. Multi-paged memoranda and briefs should be copied at referring agencies.

.dq2

RESOLUTION

WHEREAS, there are a large number of low income residents in the Chicago area who are unable to obtain civil legal services; and

WHEREAS, a 1989 Legal Needs Study authorized by the Chicago Bar Association and other bar organizations found that 80 percent of the legal needs of the poor in Illinois were not being met; and

WHEREAS, it appears that funding for the Legal Services Corporation will be reduced by 15% to 33% in 1996, which will result in a reduction in LSC funding for the Chicago area of approximately $1 million to $2 million; and

WHEREAS, The Chicago Bar Association has committed itself to increasing the provision of pro bono legal services; and

WHEREAS, The Chicago Bar Association has officially supported ABA Model Rule 6.1; and

WHEREAS, increased pro bono participation by private attorneys in the Chicago area would significantly expand the availability of legal services for the poor.

THEREFORE, it is resolved that the Chicago Bar Association:

1. Formally commit itself and its resources to increasing the availability of pro bono legal services for low income residents in the Chicago area; and

2. Adopt a suggested standard for each of its members (other than members employed as staff attorneys for

legal services organizations and members employed in government funded offices which are prohibited from performing other legal services) to perform or support pro bono legal services by taking one of the following actions:

A. Participate in a Chicago Bar Association or Chicago Bar Foundation recognized pro bono program and/or a court assignment system which results in the member representing an indigent client or clients for a minimum of 50 hours each year; or

B. Contribute a minimum of $500 per year to an agency or organization which has, as its principal purpose, the provision of legal services to low income residents of the Chicago area; or

C. As a third alternative, a member may elect to provide some amount of pro bono service below the 50 hour minimum and complete his or her commitment by a financial contribution.

3. Adopt a suggested standard for each of its members employed as staff attorneys for legal services organizations or employed by government funded offices to cooperate with and facilitate pro bono service by private attorneys.

4. Continue to make available a staff person or persons to coordinate The Chicago Bar Association's pro bono activities.

2G

THE FLORIDA BAR

FOR FEES ONLY
P.O. BOX 30381
TAMPA, FLORIDA 33630-3381
1-904-561-5832 (MEMBERSHIP RECORDS ONLY)
1-800-342-8060 • Ext. 5832

Return this copy with fee payment

ANNUAL FEE STATEMENT

☐ Please remove my name from all but required Florida Bar mailings. I otherwise understand that my address must be released in response to any properly-styled public records request.

I. IF ADDRESS HAS CHANGED, PLEASE GIVE NEW INFORMATION

MAILING ADDRESS	PHYSICAL ADDRESS (REQUIRED IF MAILING ADDRESS IS A P.O. BOX)
BUSINESS PHONE NUMBER	

II. TRUST ACCOUNT COMPLIANCE CERTIFICATE FOR JULY 1, 1995 - JUNE 30, 1996 YEAR.

Pursuant to Chapter 5 – Rules Regulating Trust Accounts; Rule 4-1.5, Fees for Legal Services; and Rule 4-1.15, Safekeeping Property – Rules Regulating The Florida Bar:

I certify that: Last year, I or my firm complied with all applicable portions of the rules with respect to the requirement for having and maintaining Florida trust accounts (including IOTA accounts, if applicable).

Date ____________________ Signature ______________________________

III. PRO BONO REPORTING FOR JULY 1, 1995 - JUNE 30, 1996 YEAR

Pursuant to Rule 4–6.1(d), Rules Regulating The Florida Bar

1. I have personally provided _____ hours of pro bono legal services: a. ☐ through an organized legal aid program; b. ☐ on my own.
2. My firm provided pro bono services collectively under a plan with the _____ Circuit Pro Bono Committee and I was allocated _____ hours.
3. I have contributed $_______ to a legal aid organization.
4. _____ I have not provided pro bono legal services to the poor this year or made a contribution to a legal aid organization.
5. During the reporting period, I was not subject to the provision of pro bono legal services to the poor because I am: (choose one) a. _____ a member of the judiciary; b. _____ judicial staff; c. _____ a governmental lawyer prohibited by statute, rule or regulation from providing services; d. _____ retired, or e. _____ inactive.
6. None of the above applies to me, but I have provided legal services to the poor in the following special manner: (see instructions)

IV. SECTION AND DIVISION DUES

☐ $20 Administrative Law (11)
☐ $25 Appellate Practice & Advocacy (21)
☐ $30 Business Law (04)
☐ $20 Criminal Law (09)
☐ $30 Elder Law (19)
☐ $25 Entertainment, Arts & Sports Law (15)
☐ $25 Environmental & Land Use Law (10)
☐ $25 Family Law (06)
☐ $20 General Practice (05)
☐ $25 Government Lawyer (18)
☐ $25 Health Law (16)
☐ $25 International Law (14)
☐ $40 Joint Dues of Gov't Lawyer/Criminal Law Section (22)
☐ $25 Labor & Employment Law (13)
☐ $25 Local Government Law (07)
☐ $20 Out-of-State Practitioners Division (20)
☐ $25 Practice Management & Development (12)
☐ $25 Public Interest Law (17)
☐ $25 Real Property Probate & Trust Law (02)
☐ $25 Tax (01)
☐ $35 Trial Lawyers (03)
☐ $25 Workers' Compensation (08)

TOTAL SECTION DUES PAID $ ________

V. VOLUNTARY CONTRIBUTIONS

F.L.A.M.E. (Florida Lawyers Association for the Maintenance of Excellence, Inc.) .... (suggested contribution – mark box) ☐ $ 25.00

THE FLORIDA BAR FOUNDATION, INC. .... (suggested contribution – mark box) ☒ $ ________

VI. MEMBERSHIP FEES

FEES ARE DUE AND PAYABLE JULY 1, 1996

Fees postmarked after **8-15-96** are assessed a $25.00 late charge. Fees postmarked after **9-30-96** are considered delinquent. A delinquent attorney is prohibited from the practice of law in Florida and from rendering advice on matters of Florida law until a $25.00 late charge, a $50.00 reinstatement fee and a petition for reinstatement is received and approved by the Board of Governors.

ANNUAL FEES

1. Prorated fee: (Balance of prorated fee for new admittees only) .... $ ________
2. Active fee: .... $ 190.00
3. Inactive fee: ($140.00) Payment must be postmarked by August 15, 1996 and election signed by attorney below. By signing below, I hereby elect inactive status under Rule 1-7.3(d). .... $ ________

   Signature: ______________________________

Payment Options: **Single payment:** Pay entire balance of lines 1 and 2 or 3 .... $ ________

OR **Installment** .... $ ________

Note: Restricted to nonelected government employees required to maintain membership in good standing **OR** attorneys in their second or third Florida Bar fiscal year of admission (Fiscal year 7-1-95 – 6-30-96). To choose installment option, payment must be postmarked by **August 15, 1996.** Other payments are due November 1, 1996 and February 1, 1997. For further information see Rule 1-7.3(c).
Computation of installment: Add lines 1 (if applicable) and 2 or 3 and divide sum by 3.

PRIOR YEAR FEES .... $ ________

DISCIPLINARY COSTS .... $ ________

Part IV ________ + Part V ________ + Part VI ________ = TOTAL AMOUNT PAID $ ________

2H

SUPREME COURT OF TEXAS

Statement of State Bar of Texas Membership Fee
June 1, 1995 - May 31, 1996

Make check, for amount of DUES only, payable to
Clerk, Supreme Court of Texas
or charge: VISA ☐ Mastercard ☐

ACCOUNT NUMBER EXP. DATE

SIGNATURE

(DO NOT MAIL ANY PORTION OF THIS STATEMENT TO THE SUPREME COURT OF TEXAS.)

TO ENSURE PROPER CREDIT, PLEASE RETURN THIS STATEMENT WITH YOUR REMITTANCE BY JUNE 1, 1995

Our records indicate that your fee for 1995-1996 is $ ________.

Please do not include Sections Dues with the Clerk's payment.

SEE REVERSE FOR 1995-1996 DUES STRUCTURE

ANNUAL PRO BONO REPORTING FORM

In the box provided, please enter the total number of hours in .25 hour increments.
Be sure to completely blacken the numbers corresponding to your entry in each column.

On May 28, 1992, the State Bar Board adopted a pro bono policy setting an aspirational goal of 50 hours of pro bono legal services to the poor for each Texas attorney each year. This form has been developed to provide the opportunity to report qualifying service. Qualifying services are:

a) the direct provision of legal services to the poor, without an expectation of compensation, whether civil or criminal,
b) uncompensated services related to simplifying the legal process for, or increasing the availability and quality of legal services to, poor persons.
c) uncompensated legal services rendered to charitable, public interest organizations with respect to matters or projects designed predominantly to address the needs of poor persons,
d) uncompensated legislative, administrative or systems advocacy services provided on behalf of poor persons; or
e) unsolicited, involuntary appointed representation of indigents in criminal and civil matters.

Neither the 50 hour standard nor this voluntary reporting form is mandatory.

For the preceding twelve months, please estimate the total number of hours of pro bono services you performed that fall within the definition shown. (Calculate in .25 hour increments.)

0	0	0	0	0	0
1	1	1	1	1	1
2	2	2	2	2	2
3	3	3	3	3	3
4	4	4	4	4	4
5	5	5	5	5	5
6	6	6	6	6	6
7	7	7	7	7	7
8	8	8	8	8	8
9	9	9	9	9	9

For more information on the definition of pro bono and the Bar's pro bono policy, call Texas Lawyers Care at 463-1463 ext. 2155 (in Austin) or toll free at (800)204-2222. Please note that pro bono services reported to a local bar program or bar association are not reported to the State Bar on your behalf.

IOLTA/Texas Equal Access to Justice Foundation

ANNUAL IOLTA (Interest on Lawyers' Trust Accounts) COMPLIANCE STATEMENT - DUE JULY 1, 1995

Texas attorneys are required to submit annually an IOLTA Compliance Statement. Information about your current IOLTA status is printed below. Please verify that the information is accurate. Use the reverse side of form to make any changes. Please sign the IOLTA Compliance Statement and return in the enclosed envelope. **IF YOU FAIL TO DO SO, YOUR LICENSE TO PRACTICE LAW IN THE STATE OF TEXAS MAY BE SUBJECT TO SUSPENSION.**

UNT NUMBER ACCOUNT NAME ATTORNEY SIGNATURE REQUIRED FOR VALIDATION

SIGNATURE DATE

RESOLUTION

Whereas, on October 27, 1995, the Board of Managers of the Chicago Bar Association (CBA) approved a resolution that adopted a suggested standard for its 22,000 members to render at least 50 hours of pro bono legal services per year or make a contribution of at least $500 to an organization that provides legal services to low income residents of the Chicago area;

Whereas, the pro bono suggested standard adopted by the CBA's Board of Managers is based on the ABA Model Rule 6.1 ("Voluntary Pro Bono Publico Service") which the CBA has officially supported;

Whereas, the CBA had also approved on August 14, 1986 a similar resolution to that of October 27, 1995, but to date has never attempted to ascertain empirically whether its members are meeting the CBA's recommended minimum levels of pro bono activity;

Whereas, the reduced funding by Congress of legal services programs for the poor threatens to enlarge the already well documented unmet legal needs of the poor in the Chicago area;

Whereas, an administrative mechanism exists for the CBA to request annually that its members voluntarily report on the approximate number of pro bono hours they have spent and contributions they have made;

Whereas, the data obtained from these reports would serve to: remind CBA members of their obligation to provide pro bono legal services to low income persons; assist the CBA to determine whether members are meeting its minimum suggested pro bono standards; and provide an information base for the CBA to explore future strategies to encourage pro bono legal services;

Therefore, it is resolved that the Chicago Bar Association:

1. Mail to its members once a year a voluntary reporting form returnable to the CBA in a self-addressed, stamped envelope to allow each member to estimate, among other things, the number of hours spent in the prior year on pro bono legal services and the amount of contributions made to agencies that provide legal services to low income residents in the Chicago area (see attached Voluntary Pro Bono Activity Report).

2. Prepare a report to its members each year based in part on the data obtained from the returned voluntary forms and submit recommendations, if appropriate, on additional measures to encourage its members to meet their professional obligation to provide pro bono legal services.

Passed by the CBA Board of Managers, March 7, 1996

Chicago Bar Association

Voluntary Pro Bono Activity Report

On October 27, 1995, the CBA Board of Managers approved a resolution adopting a suggested standard for its members of a minimum of 50 hours of pro bono legal services per year or a contribution of at least $500 to an organization that provides legal services to low income persons living in the Chicago area. This report has been developed and approved by the CBA Board of Managers to assess qualifying pro bono service on an annual basis.

Whether or not you performed pro bono or contributed money to legal services in 1995, your individual response will assist the CBA in assessing the extent to which CBA members are contributing to their communities and to the profession. The data obtained from this report should also be helpful in counteracting the negative image of the legal profession, by quantifying the amount of pro bono activity done by CBA members. All replies can be anonymous. Please take a moment to fill out the report and return it to the Chicago Bar Association, 321 S. Plymouth Court, Chicago, IL 60604-3997, or **via fax at 312/554-2054, by April 26, 1996**.

Neither meeting the 50 hour/$500 standard nor completing this reporting form is mandatory.

Please answer the questions on the reverse side of this form based on calendar year 1995. For each question, check the box that applies and where indicated, provide the follow-up information requested. When applicable, fill in the blanks with the specific information requested. Use ABA Model Rule 6.1, officially supported by the CBA, as a guide. The Rule states:

> **"A lawyer should aspire to render at least (50) hours of pro bono publico legal services per year. In fulfilling this responsibility, the lawyer should:**
>
> **(a) provide a substantial majority of the (50) hours of legal services without fee or expectation of fee to:**
>
> **(1) persons of limited means or**
>
> **(2) charitable, religious, civic, community, governmental and educational organizations in matters which are designed primarily to address the needs of persons of limited means; and**
>
> **(b) provide any additional services through:**
>
> **(1) delivery of legal services at no fee or substantially reduced fee to individuals, groups or organizations seeking to secure or protect civil rights, civil liberties or public rights, or charitable, religious, civic, community, governmental and educational organizations in matters in furtherance of their organizational purposes, where the payment of standard legal fees would significantly deplete the organization's economic resources or would be otherwise inappropriate;**
>
> **(2) delivery of legal services at a substantially reduced fee to persons of limited means; or**
>
> **(3) participation in activities for improving the law, the legal system or the legal profession.**
>
> **In addition, a lawyer should voluntarily contribute financial support to organizations that provide legal services to persons of limited means."**

CBA
Voluntary Pro Bono Activity Report

1. During calendar year 1995, I represented, without expectation of compensation, individuals with limited means referred to me from a legal services organization (e.g., Chicago Volunteer Legal Services, Volunteer Lawyers for the Homeless, Chicago Legal Clinic, Legal Clinic for the Disabled, any CBA - or Chicago Bar Foundation-recognized pro bono program, etc.) (Sec. (a)(l) of ABA Model Rule 6.1 - on flipside):

❒ yes: No. of cases accepted ______
No. of hours spent on those cases ______
❒ no

2. During 1995, I represented, without expectation of compensation from the onset of such representation, individuals of limited means *without* the involvement of a legal services organization (Sec. (a)(1) of ABA Model Rule 6.1):

❒ yes: No. of cases accepted ______
No. of hours spent on those cases ______
❒ no

3. During 1995, without expectation of compensation, I spent time providing legal services for non-profit organizations in matters designed primarily to address the needs of persons of limited means (Sec. (a)(2) of ABA Model Rule 6.1):

❒ yes: No. of hours spent ______
❒ no

4. During 1995, I spent time providing services in activities not included in questions 1-3 but described in Sections (b)(1),(2) and (3) of ABA Model Rule 6.1 above:

❒ yes: No. of hours spent ______
Describe services rendered: ______________________
____
❒ no

5. During 1995, I was not able to provide pro bono legal services because I was (choose one):

❒ a member of judiciary ❒ judicial staff
❒ a government lawyer prohibited by statute, rule or regulation from providing services
❒ discouraged by my employer ❒ retired ❒ inactive
❒ other: ______________________________

6. During 1995, the money I gave to legal services, pro bono, or other organizations providing legal services to low income persons was $______.

7. The size of my office is (choose one):

❒ sole practitioner ❒ 16-50 lawyers
❒ 2-5 lawyers ❒ over 50 lawyers
❒ 6-15 lawyers ❒ I do not practice law

8. My regular work is primarily in the following subject-matter area(s):

❒ administrative ❒ employment law
❒ bankruptcy ❒ environmental law
❒ business/commercial ❒ estate planning/probate
❒ civil litigation ❒ family law
❒ civil rights ❒ government
❒ criminal law ❒ immigration
❒ corporate counsel ❒ worker's compensation
❒ other ______________________________

9. The number of years I have been in practice: ____

10. (*Optional*) My customary hourly fee: $________

Other comments/suggestions: ________________
____
____
____
(Use additional paper if necessary)

(Optional): Name ______________________
Address ______________________________
____
______________ Phone ______________
Fax ______________ Email ______________

***For more information** on the definition of pro bono, the CBA's pro bono policy, or CBA-recognized pro bono opportunities, please call Linda Rio, Director of Community Service at the Chicago Bar Association, at 312/294-9611.*

❒ *Please check this box if you would like to receive the Chicago Bar Foundation brochure on pro bono opportunities in the Chicago area (address needed above).*
4/96

See other side for Rule and explanation

SECTION 3

SECTION 3: SUPPORT OF PRO BONO PROGRAMS AND ACTIVITIES

This section of the handbook addresses methods through which the bar can support existing pro bono programs operated by other organizations. Section 4 deals with situations in which the bar association directly operates a pro bono program.

Recruiting For Pro Bono Programs

Discussion

Because bar associations include attorneys from a wide range of backgrounds and practice areas, bar association networks provide unique opportunities for the recruitment of pro bono attorneys. It is important to note, however, that volunteers should not be recruited until pro bono programs are in place that can immediately use volunteers.

Bar luncheons and other gatherings present ideal occasions for bar leaders to educate members about the need for pro bono services. Recruiting materials can be included in bar magazines and notices of meetings and events. Meetings of committees and sections provide additional opportunities for the recruitment of pro bono attorneys. Many bar associations sponsor annual pro bono recruiting campaigns. These campaigns frequently are initiated through a letter to all bar members signed by the Chief Judge and/or the bar president. The letter encourages bar members to participate in an organized pro bono program, and often is accompanied by a brochure describing the program, along with an enrollment card to be returned.

Some bar associations sponsor special recruiting events, such as telethons, where volunteer attorneys call other attorneys to solicit their involvement in an organized pro bono program. In other cases, bar leaders may request particular sections to handle certain types of pro bono cases, such as bankruptcy, consumer law, family law or real property. Sections also may be approached to start clinics for clients. Finally, law firms, corporate counsel offices and government attorney offices can be encouraged to take on specific pro bono projects, including conducting client intake on certain days or nights, forming a "conflicts" panel, handling transactional cases (e.g. the legal work necessary to develop affordable housing projects; the incorporation of not-for-profit organizations that benefit persons of limited means), or putting together educational materials regarding particular areas of law (e.g. child support, used car purchases, debtor's rights).

In predominantly rural states, recruiting often is done on a statewide basis. A statewide panel can provide pro bono resources for rural areas through matching attorneys in larger counties with clients in smaller counties. State bar leaders or state pro bono support directors may travel from one bar association to another in an effort to recruit attorneys for a statewide pro bono panel, or involvement on a local panel. Bar associations in rural counties often lack the organizational structure to support an organized pro bono program. In these situations, it may be advisable for judges and bar leaders to recruit pro bono attorneys on a more informal basis.

Pros

- ☞ Bar events and networks provide excellent opportunities for recruiting pro bono attorneys.
- ☞ Statewide recruitment allows for the distribution of pro bono resources on a statewide basis.

Cons

- ☞ Recruiting may be administratively intensive.
- ☞ Recruiting efforts may require the expenditure of funds for mailing, printing of brochures, travel, etc.

Contacts

South Carolina Bar Pro Bono Program
Staff Contact: Donna Stobbe, Executive Director ((803) 799-6653
Volunteer Contact: George Cauthen (803) 733-9404

H.A.V.E. A HEART Program (Tampa, Florida)
Staff Contact: Sheila Griffin (813) 229-9156 x 139
Volunteer Contact: Honorable James M. Barton II (813) 272-5778

Examples

South Carolina Bar Pro Bono Program Enrollment Brochure (Attachment 3-A)

H.A.V.E. A HEART Recruiting Brochure and Enrollment Form (Attachment 3-B)

Provision of Malpractice Insurance

Discussion

Bar associations should consider providing malpractice insurance to attorneys rendering pro bono services. In many cases, pro bono attorneys are covered through their law firm's policy, or by the policy of a pro bono program with which they are affiliated. Certain groups of attorneys, however, including government attorneys, may not be covered. Bar associations should attempt to provide malpractice insurance to address any gap areas that exist. The provision of malpractice insurance is an important recruiting tool, as well as an important element of quality control of legal services.

Pros

- ☞ The provision of malpractice insurance is an incentive to pro bono participation.
- ☞ The provision of malpractice insurance increases quality control of legal services.

Cons

- ☞ Malpractice insurance policies may be costly.

Contacts

State Bar of Michigan
Staff Contact: Mike Karwoski (517) 372-9033 x 3017

Fundraising for Pro Bono Programs

Discussion

Bar associations sponsor a variety of fundraising efforts for pro bono programs. Some bar associations organize annual fundraising campaigns; others sponsor special events such as telethons, charity balls, golf tournaments, or fashion shows. Bar associations also seek grants, funding from the state legislature, and filing fee surcharges to finance pro bono activities. The

ABA publication: *Innovative Fundraising Ideas for Legal Services* provides a variety of fundraising ideas applicable to bar associations. Please refer to this publication for further information.

Pros

- ☞ Bar associations are likely to have the organizational structure and resources to sponsor fundraising efforts.

Cons

- ☞ Special fundraising events are extremely labor-intensive.
- ☞ Certain special events are very costly.

Contacts

Volunteer Legal Services Project, Monroe County (New York)
Fundraising Phonathon
Staff Contact: Hanna Cohn, Executive Director (716) 232-3051
Volunteer Contact: Brian Zorn (716) 423-5900

Legal Aid Society of Palm Beach County (Florida)
Fundraising Fashion Show, Auction and Recognition Evening
Staff Contact: Joan Krug (407) 655-8944 x 258

New Orleans Pro Bono Project "Justice For All" Ball
Staff Contact: Rachel Piercey, Executive Director (504) 581-4043
Volunteer Contact: David F. Bienvenu (504) 523-1385

Examples

Volunteer Legal Services Project, Monroe County, Fundraising Phonathon (Attachment 3-C)

New Orleans "Justice For All" Ball (Attachment 3-D)

Training Pro Bono Attorneys

Discussion

Training is a vital aspect of recruiting pro bono attorneys. It also increases the level of quality control of legal services to clients of pro bono programs. Many attorneys are reluctant to handle pro bono cases involving legal matters outside of their practice area. Training is an incentive that bar associations can offer to encourage attorneys to handle pro bono cases. Bar associations provide training in a variety of ways. Some bars offer free CLE programs directed at recruiting pro bono attorneys for certain types of cases. Other bars offer discounts on CLE programs to attorneys who accept pro bono referrals. Attorneys benefit by obtaining CLE credits without charge. Pro bono programs benefit by recruiting additional panel members. Some bar associations sponsor training clinics for certain types of cases, such as family law and bankruptcy. Clinics enable pro bono attorneys to meet in small groups with program staff to review specific cases, and learn basis procedural and substantive principles of the areas of law involved.

Practice sections also may offer training seminars geared toward the pro bono attorney. Sections of family law, bankruptcy, litigation, probate and estate planning, guardianship and real property are particularly appropriate because the legal problems of persons of limited means frequently fall within these practice areas. Sections also can be called upon to prepare written training materials for pro bono attorneys relating to specific areas of law.

Finally, mentoring is an effective tool for training pro bono attorneys. Experienced attorneys with specialized expertise can mentor or co-counsel pro bono cases with less-experienced attorneys. Mentoring is a creative way to promote pro bono activity within law firms (senior partner mentoring new associate) or practice sections.

Pros

☞ Training provides a direct incentive for the recruitment of pro bono attorneys.

☞ Training increases the level of quality control of legal services delivered to pro bono program clients.

Cons

☞ Training can be labor-intensive.

☞ Training may involve financial expenditures or loss of revenue when free CLE training is offered to pro bono attorneys.

Contacts

State Bar of Georgia
Staff Contact: Ayres Gardner, State Pro Bono Support Director (404) 527-8762
Volunteer Contact: Benjamin F. Easterlin, IV (912) 924-9316

New Hampshire Bar Association
Staff Contact: Joanne Lang, CLE Director (603) 224-6942
Volunteer Contact: Kevin Devine (603) 668-5888

The Virginia State Bar
Staff Contacts: Maureen Petrini, Virginia State Bar Pro Bono Coordinator (804)775-0522
David Rubinstein, Executive Director, Virginia Poverty Law Center
(804) 782-9430

Volunteer Legal Services Program of the Bar Association of San Francisco
Staff Contact: Tanya Neiman, Executive Director (415) 267-0715

Examples

Article on Family Law Training Clinics, Volunteer Legal Services Program of the Bar Association of San Francisco (Attachment 3-E)

Materials from Training Seminars Sponsored by the Virginia State Bar and Bar Association of the City of Richmond (Attachment 3-F)

Sponsorship of Pro Bono Recognition and Awards

Discussion

Bar-sponsored awards and recognition events are an ideal occasion for recognizing outstanding pro bono efforts of attorneys and judges. The public recognition of bar members who have made outstanding pro bono contributions results in multiple benefits. First, it is an effective recruiting tool. Awards events encourage and inspire other attorneys to participate in pro bono programs. Further, recognition events present valuable opportunities for bar associations to improve public relations with the community. Media representatives should be invited to awards and recognition events, and provided with information about the bar's pro bono commitment prior to the event. Finally, and perhaps most importantly, pro bono attorneys deserve recognition and should be thanked publicly.

Some bar associations include the recognition of pro bono attorneys as part of a general awards ceremony. For example, many local bar associations observe "Law Day" each year, and include pro bono awards as a part of the program. State bars may recognize pro bono attorneys at awards ceremonies held during annual or mid-year meetings. Other bars host recognition events solely for the purpose of recognizing pro bono attorneys.

An annual "Pro Bono Recognition" lunch or dinner provides an opportunity for bar leaders to publicly thank attorneys who have contributed time or money to pro bono programs. The names of attorneys and law firms that have made outstanding pro bono contributions can be printed in the program, with an indication of how many hours were contributed, or a description of a particularly outstanding case result. In some communities, awards are given in particular categories, including: "Most Pro Bono Hours Contributed by an Individual Attorney;" "Outstanding Case Result;" "Greatest Number of Hours Contributed by a Law Firm;" or "Outstanding Pro Bono Project by a Government Attorney Office."

Pros

- ☞ Awards events are an ideal opportunity to publicly recognize and thank pro bono attorneys for their efforts.
- ☞ Awards events encourage and inspire other attorneys to participate in pro bono programs.
- ☞ Awards events improve the bar's public image with the media and the community at large.

Cons

- ☞ Awards events require significant planning.
- ☞ Awards events may be costly.
- ☞ Insular awards events may be poorly attended.

Contacts

American Bar Association
Standing Committee on Lawyers' Public Service Responsibility
Staff Contact: Dorothy Jackson (312) 988-5766
Volunteer Contact: James L. Baillie (612) 347-7013

New Hampshire Bar Association
Staff Contact: Jeannine McCoy, Executive Director (603) 224-6942
Volunteer Contact: L. Jonathan Ross (603) 669-2211

H.A.V.E. A HEART Program (Tampa, Florida)
Staff Contact: Sheila Griffin, Director, Bay Area Volunteer Lawyers Program
(813) 229-9156, ext. 139
Volunteer Contacts: Honorable James M. Barton II (813) 272-5778
William Reece Smith (813) 223-7000

Justice For All Awards Dinner, San Diego Volunteer Lawyer Program
Staff Contact: Carl Poirot, Executive Director (619) 235-5656 x 108
Volunteer Contact: Stephen F. Yunker (619) 233-5500

Examples

Nomination Brochure for ABA Pro Bono Publico Awards (Attachment 3-G)

Brochure for Justice For All Awards Dinner, San Diego Volunteer Lawyer Program (Attachment 3-H)

Commitment of Bar's Public Relations Resources

Discussion

Bar associations can be an effective conduit for funneling information to the media about pro bono activities. Most bars constantly seek positive press. Publicity about pro bono activities is an ideal method for demonstrating the good works of attorneys in the community.

Large bar associations often employ a staff person to coordinate public relations and media coverage. If so, this person should become familiar with the various pro bono efforts of bar members. It is advisable to include this staff person in planning awards and recognition events, and to utilize his or her press contacts in preparing invitation lists. In addition, this staff person should be encouraged to provide information about bar members' pro bono activities to the media on a regular basis.

In smaller bar associations where there is no public relations staff, volunteers and other staff members should routinely inform the media about pro bono activities. Bar members also should write columns in the bar magazine to educate readers about the need for pro bono attorneys, and to recognize outstanding pro bono efforts of bar members. In some communities, public relations specialists volunteer their time to assist bar associations with public service projects.

Pros

- ☞ Use of the bar's public relations resources is a relatively easy and inexpensive way to increase recognition of pro bono attorneys and recruit additional pro bono attorneys.
- ☞ Pro bono activity is a source of positive press for bar associations.

Cons

- ☞ Preparation of press releases and other public relations strategies can be time-consuming.

Contacts

Volunteer Legal Services Project of Monroe County (New York)
Staff Contact: Hanna Cohn, Executive Director (716) 232-3051
Volunteer Contact: Brian Zorn (716) 423-5900

San DiegoVolunteer Lawyer Program (California)
Staff Contact: Carl Poirot, Executive Director (619) 235-5656

SECTION 3 ATTACHMENTS

Pro Bono Works for Lawyers . . .

- **Professional Liability Insurance:** For all pro bono referrals.
- **S.C. Bar CLE Vouchers:** Awarded to attorneys who complete 35 or more hours of pro bono service.
- **Litigation Support:** Volunteer court reporters, psychologists, law school students and process servers.
- **Litigation Fund:** For some costs and expenses.
- **Library Resources:** Located at the six legal services offices.
- **Pro Bono Credit:** For civil court appointed cases and direct intakes.
- **Recognition:** South Carolina Bar annual service awards. Certificates of Appreciation. Annual Pro Bono Honor Roll.
- **Right of Refusal:** At any time for any reason.

The South Carolina Bar Pro Bono Program

Providing access to justice for indigent South Carolinians

South Carolina Bar Pro Bono Program

The Pro Bono Program stimulates and supports volunteer work by the private bar. Training courses, materials, streamlined administration, malpractice insurance and administrative support help private lawyers make efficient and rewarding use of their pro bono time. The program is committed to continuing the delivery of legal representation to our state's indigent population through volunteer lawyer participation. We are also committed to identifying and implementing innovative and efficient service delivery systems.

Poor people need a lawyer's advice and representation for a variety of problems. Some problems relate to basic necessities such as food, shelter and health care. There are also problems shared with more affluent people, such as those concerning domestic relations, education, consumer issues, employment and individual rights. The difference is that low-income people do not have the resources to pay for the legal help they need.

In South Carolina, 16.4% or 582,000 people live below the poverty level. That's 34,000 more than in 1990. Legal Services statewide has a mere 55 attorneys to address the legal needs of our state's indigent population. Alone, Legal Services could not possibly accomplish the task. The Pro Bono Program is sponsored by the South Carolina Bar and the South Carolina Legal Services agencies. This working partnership maximizes the common effort for the public good and helps to close the gap between the legal needs of the poor and the legal resources available.

All pro bono clients must meet federally established poverty income guidelines. In order for clients to take advantage of the legal services provided by the South Carolina Bar Program they must first contact their local legal services agency.

For more information about the South Carolina Bar Pro Bono Program call 1-800-395-3425 or, if you are in the Columbia area, 799-4015.

Become a Pro Bono Volunteer

Name________________________

Address______________________

____

Phone________________________

Please check one:

___I will donate 50 hours of time over 12 months.

___I will donate___ volunteer hours over 12 months and make a financial contribution of $__________.

___I am unable to donate time but will support the Pro Bono Program with a contribution of at least $250.

Complete and mail to:

South Carolina Bar
Pro Bono Program
Post Office Box 608
Columbia, SC 29202

HAVE

...a heart

Hillsborough
Attorneys
Volunteer
Efforts

Administered by Bay Area Legal Services Volunteer Lawyers Program

H.A.V.E. A HEART PROGRAM

H.A.V.E. A HEART is the pro bono program of the Thirteenth Judicial Circuit of Florida. The program has been approved by the Circuit Pro Bono Committee, and it is administered by Bay Area Legal Services. Active participation in the program provides lawyers with opportunities to fulfill their professional obligation to assist persons who cannot afford to pay for legal services. Attorneys can volunteer their services in a number of ways, as described below. Every effort will be made to accommodate volunteers' preferences. However, due to the extraordinary demand for legal assistance in family law, we encourage lawyers to volunteer in that area. Training materials and mentors in the family law area are available.

Program Description

1) **Case Referral Panel** - Volunteers agree to accept case referrals in designated areas from Bay Area Legal Services and the Guardian Ad Litem program. Clients are screened for eligibility and legal merit prior to referral.
2) **Intake** - Volunteers assist with initial client interviews and eligibility screening. For general civil intake, priority is given to government lawyers, corporate counsel and other attorneys who are unable to accept case referrals.
3) **Self-Help Divorce Clinic** - Volunteers assist clients in a clinic setting with divorce pleadings in cases where there are no minor children, joint property or liabilities.
4) **Project to Assist Homeless Persons** - Volunteers interview clients at homeless shelters, and perform legal follow-up as needed.
5) **Project to Assist Farmworkers** - Volunteers interview farmworker clients at the Bethel Mission in Wimauma.
6) **Project to Assist Persons with AIDS** - Volunteers represent HIV-positive clients and persons with AIDS with various legal problems related to their medical condition.
7) **Community Counsel** - Volunteers provide legal assistance to community groups or non-profit organizations whose mission is to assist low-income persons (including affordable housing and community redevelopment projects).
8) **Teen Court** - Volunteers serve as judges in the teen court program, a diversionary program for juvenile first offenders.
9) **Courthouse Assistance Project** - Volunteers assist walk-in clients at the County Courthouse with form pleadings and other legal questions.
10) **Haitian Political Asylum Project** - Volunteers prepare political asylum candidates for INS hearings.
11) **Mediation** - Trained volunteer mediators train students as Peer Mediators in the public schools, and mediate juvenile dependency and family law matters.
12) **Speakers' Bureau** - Volunteers speak to client groups at various outreach locations on legal issues affecting low-income persons.
13) **Client Education** - Volunteers develop brochures regarding legal problems affecting low-income persons (e.g. buying a used car, debt collection, name changes). This project is well-suited for a government office or corporate counsel.
14) **Legal Research** - Volunteers provide legal research for Bay Area Legal Services staff attorneys.
15) **Attorneys Fighting for Seriously Ill Children** - Volunteers advise families of children with life-threatening illnesses on matters involving employee insurance benefits, wills and estate planning, and debt and financial problems.
16) **Income Tax Assistance Project** - Trained volunteers advise and assist needy individuals and families in preparation and filing of tax returns (e.g. assistance of homeless persons who are currently employed and may be entitled to substantial tax benefits).
17) **Hospice Project** - Volunteers assist terminally ill Hospice patients and their families with legal problems. Hospital and home visits may be required.
18) **Victim Restitution Project** - Volunteers assist victims of crime in obtaining and enforcing restitution judgements against their assailants.
19) **Military Assistance Project** - Volunteers provide legal assistance to veterans and military personnel.
20) **Criminal Law Panel** - Volunteers handle criminally-related cases that cannot result in conviction (e.g. post conviction relief, expungements, driving offenses.)

Program Benefits

The program supports volunteers in the following ways:

- Professional liability coverage is provided to all volunteer attorneys who handle cases on behalf of Bay Area Legal Services. This includes coverage for intake attorneys as well as attorneys who represent clients. The coverage is secondary to any other coverage the attorney may have.
- Volunteers receive resource materials to enable them to represent indigent clients.
- Group and individual training is conducted upon request.
- Costs of litigation and other case-related costs can be paid by Bay Areas Legal Services when reasonable and necessary.
- Bay Area Legal Services tracks the number of hours of pro bono service performed by its volunteers. These records will be made available to volunteer attorneys for reporting to the Florida Bar.

How To Join

Simply complete the attached enrollment card and return to:

H.A.V.E. A HEART Bay Area Volunteer Lawyers Program, 700 Twiggs Street, Suite 800, Tampa, Florida 33602, (813) 223-2525.

H.A.V.E. A HEART ENROLLMENT CARD

Count me in to participate in the following ways:

1) I prefer case referrals in the following practice areas:

FAMILY LAW

_____ Dissolution of Marriage and Custody
_____ Post-Judgment Relief
_____ Adoption
_____ Name Changes
_____ Attorney Ad Litem
_____ Guardian Ad Litem
_____ Mentoring

JUVENILE DEPENDENCY

_____ Defending parents in dependency or termination proceedings
_____ Representing non-parents seeking custody in dependency or termination proceedings

_____ **GUARDIANSHIP**
_____ **PROBATE**

REAL PROPERTY

_____ Litigation
_____ Transactional

_____ **BANKRUPTCY**
_____ **CONSUMER PROTECTION** (Contract disputes,including unfair sales practices, used car sales, repairs)
_____ **LIFE AND HEALTH INSURANCE MATTERS**

APPEALS

_____ Civil
_____ Administrative

_____ **EMPLOYMENT** (generally, representing employees)
_____ **AUTOMOBILE NEGLIGENCE AND INSURANCE MATTERS** (generally, non-fee generating)
_____ **IMMIGRATION**
_____ **TAX**
_____ **FEDERAL CIVIL RIGHTS LITIGATION**
_____ **OTHER** (please indicate)

2) General Civil Intake (Downtown Tampa)

_____ Wednesday evenings (5:30 p.m. - 8:00 p.m.)
_____ Saturday mornings (9:00 a.m. - 12:00 p.m.)

3) _____ Plant City Intake (one day a month, to be determined)

4) _____ Family Law Intake (one evening a month, to be determined)

5) _____ Self-Help Divorce Clinic (one day a month, to be determined)

6) _____ Project to Assist Homeless Persons

7) _____ Project to Assist Farmworkers

8) _____ Project to Assist Persons with AIDS

9) _____ Income Tax Assistance Project

10) _____ Hospice Project

11) _____ Victim Restitution Project

12) _____ Military Assistance Project

13) _____ Attorneys Fighting for Seriously Ill Children Project

14) _____ Community Counsel

15) _____ Teen Court

16) _____ Courthouse Assistance Project

17) _____ Criminal Law Panel

18) _____ Haitian Political Asylum Project

19) _____ Mediation

_____ Peer Mediation in the Public Schools
_____ Juvenile Dependency Mediation
_____ Family Law Mediation

20) _____ Speakers' Bureau

21) _____ Client Education

22) _____ Legal Research

Place
Stamp
Here

H.A.V.E. A HEART
Bay Area Volunteer Lawyers Program
700 Twiggs Street, Suite 800
Tampa, Florida 33602-4079

ENROLLMENT

Name ______________________________

Firm ______________________________

Street ______________________________

P.O. Box ______________________________

City ______________________________

Telephone ______________________________

Year admitted to practice ____________ In Fla. ____________

Foreign language ability ______________________________

VLSP Phonathon – Give A Call

by Hanna Cohn, Esq., Director
Volunteer Legal Services Project of Monroe County

Call it "getting to yes" or "impossible to say no": Volunteer Legal Services Project of Monroe County Inc. (VLSP) in Rochester, New York has learned that a phonathon is an excellent way to raise money for *pro bono* programs.

Since 1986, VLSP has conducted a phonathon to raise money for the program's operating expenses. The target audience for phonathon calls is the entire bench and bar in Monroe County.

Why A Phonathon?

Originally a bar-sponsored *pro bono* program, VLSP has operated as a not-for-profit corporation since 1982. Since its inception, the agency has had a diverse funding base including a Private Attorney Involvement grant from Monroe County Legal Assistance Corporation, United Way funding, foundation support and, since 1987, Interest on Lawyer Account monies. Financial support from the legal community has also been part of the funding base since 1984.

In 1984 and 1985, VLSP conducted a direct mail solicitation of the bench and bar in Monroe County. In 1985, the mail solicitation had a 2.3 percent response rate, which is an average response for direct mail efforts. In that year, VLSP raised a total of $1,930 from individual attorneys and judges, which was supplemented by large donations from a number of law firms, for a fund drive total of $11,380.

In 1986, a professional fundraiser joined the VLSP board. She immediately began to urge the board's development committee to consider a telephone solicitation to replace the mail solicitation. There was significant resistance to the idea from both the development committee and the board for a number of reasons. First, there was aversion to telephone solicitation: no one likes making these phone calls and no one likes receiving them. Second, there was concern that individual solicitation might not raise as much as the amount that had been contributed by law firms.

The urging of VLSP's fundraiser colleague prevailed, however, and VLSP held its first phonathon in November, 1986.

Phonathon Preparation

The first phonathon effort involved a significant expenditure of staff resources. Labels with the names of nearly 2,000 members of the bar association were affixed to printed pledge cards. Home telephone numbers for the attorneys and judges were needed on each of

these cards. Fortunately, VLSP at that time had a part-time clerical aide funded under an employment training grant. This employee spent many long, tedious hours looking up the necessary telephone numbers.

VLSP found that this labor-intensive activity was necessary only in the first year of the phonathon. The same pledge cards were used in 1987. In 1988, staff transferred telephone numbers from old cards to new cards which was much less labor intensive than looking up the numbers in the phone book.

Next to preparing pledge cards, the most time consuming aspect of preparing for the phonathon is securing as many callers as possible. The core of the callers is VLSP's Board of Directors, but past presidents of the bar association, members of the bar association's board of trustees, past members of VLSP's board and many "friends of VLSP" are also invited to participate. Because the key to success in a phonathon is attorneys calling their peers, VLSP recruits callers ranging from newly admitted attorneys to bar leaders, and representing the matrimonial, real estate, tax and other bars.

VLSP advertised the phonathon in bar publications in the month preceding the phonathon and mailed a "we'll be calling you" postcard to all members of the bar a week before the event.

The Phonathon

When

VLSP holds its annual phonathon in November, in the middle of the month, before our callers get tied up in holiday activities. The solicitation seems to take place at a good time of the year for charitable gifts—prior to the end of the tax year.

Where

Members of VLSP's board have secured use of the offices of investment firms for each phonathon. Although a law firm or any office with enough trunk lines would be a suitable location for a phonathon, we have found that having callers working at a bank of phones, rather than isolated in offices, makes the phonathon more fun for callers and helps generate enthusiasm for the effort.

How

VLSP invites all callers to dinner at the phonathon location at 5:30 on the evening of the phonathon. Complicated catering is not necessary; we bring in a fancy boxed dinner from a local catering firm. At 6:30, an orientation/cheerleading session takes place. Callers are given background on VLSP's financial needs, told the goal of the evening's calling and are given tips for effective solicitation. All of this information is also contained in a calling guide that VLSP had developed.

Callers chose cards of attorneys and judges whom they feel comfortable in calling. Each card indicates previous donations that the individual has made to VLSP, so that the caller has a point of reference for a specific pledge. When a pledge is made, the caller notes the amount on the pledge card. At the same time, the caller fills out a mailing card on which she/he fills in the name and address of the donor, a salutation, the amount of the pledge and his/her signature. VLSP mails these out the following day along with a remittance envelope. In that way, the donor receives an immediate verification of and thank you for the pledge.

Success!

In the first year of VLSP's phonathon, 25 callers raised $14,200 in pledges from 268 attorneys over the course of two nights. This represents a 730% increase over the amount raised in individual donations the previous year through the mail solicitation. The phonathon has grown in number of callers and proceeds in the past five years. In 1990, nearly 50 callers raised $32,000 in pledges over the two nights of the phonathon. As in past years, several law firms decided to make firm contributions, and the attorneys in those firms were not called during the phonathon. VLSP expects to raise a total of $42,000 in pledges from the phonathon, from law firm gifts and in response to a "sorry we missed you" mailing to those who were not called during the phonathon.

In each of the VLSP phonathons, we have enrolled several new volunteers in addition to receiving significant financial support. Some attorneys have volunteered their time instead of a donation; others have volunteered both.

VLSP's extraordinary success in its phonathons has led the project to consider a similar approach for volunteer recruitment. It seems to be hard to say no to a colleague or friend; the implications for volunteer recruitment are clear.

Phonathons may not be right for every program. This fundraising technique requires significant staff resources (particularly in the first year), a committed board and hard working volunteer solicitors. Most importantly, a phonathon's success depends, at least in part, on the good will that the program has in the community.

You'll Soon Be Hearing From Us!

On the evenings of November 16 and 17, one of your colleagues will call to ask you to support the important work of Volunteer Legal Services Project. Since opening in September 1981, VLSP has assisted over 4,000 people with a wide variety of legal problems. We need the support of the legal community to maintain this important resource.

When you receive your call, please respond with a generous pledge for VLSP. If for any reason we miss you, or if you would like to contribute before the phonathon, your contribution can be sent to:

VLSP, 87 N. Clinton Avenue, Rochester, N.Y. 14604.

Volunteer Legal Services Project of Monroe County, Inc.

1990-91 Development Campaign

Dear

Thank you for your phonathon pledge of $ _______ . Please make your check payable to Volunteer Legal Services Project. VLSP is a tax exempt organization, contributions to which are deductible for N.Y. State and federal income tax purposes.

Your support is important and is sincerely appreciated.

Phonathon Checklist

Two months in advance:

Have pledge cards printed, affix labels of target audience and start to look up phone numbers

Advise board members of date, ask board to suggest other callers

Check deadlines for bar publications to advertise phonathon

Six weeks in advance:

Confirm location for phonathon

Letters out to potential callers, soliciting their participation and asking them to save date; enclose response coupon

Four weeks in advance:

Contact callers

Have pledge thank you's, remittance envelopes and window envelopes printed

Two weeks in advance:

Confirmation letters to callers

Pre-call postcard in mail

One week in advance:

Order dinners

Two days after phonathon:

Mail pledge thank you's with remittance envelope

Two weeks after phonathon:

"Sorry we missed you" letter to those not called

Start thank you letters to contributors

FIRST CARD WITH MAY 15 DEADLINE

JUSTICE FOR ALL BALL

September 8, 1995
Gallier Hall

Company Name (as will appear on invitation) ____________

____

Contact Person ____________

Address ____________

____

Telephone ____________

____ Yes, we would like to be listed as a Patron.
($1,000.00 Contribution, 8 tickets to Ball)

____ Yes, we would like to be listed as a Sponsor.
($750.00 Contribution, 6 tickets to Ball)

____ Yes, we would like to purchase tickets at $75.00 per person.

____ We cannot participate, but please accept our donation.

Enclosed is our check, made payable to the New Orleans Pro Bono Project, in the amount of $ ____________

Please respond by May 1, 1995 to ensure listing on invitation.

New Orleans Pro Bono Project
601 St. Charles Avenue • New Orleans, LA 70130
581-4043

AS A FINAL DEADLINE

JUSTICE FOR ALL BALL

September 8, 1995
Gallier Hall

Company Name (as will appear on invitation) ____________

____

Contact Person ____________

Address ____________

____

Telephone ____________

____ Yes, we would like to be listed as a Patron.
($1,000.00 Contribution, 8 tickets to Ball)

____ Yes, we would like to be listed as a Sponsor.
($750.00 Contribution, 6 tickets to Ball)

____ Yes, we would like to purchase tickets at $75.00 per person.

____ We cannot participate, but please accept our donation.

Enclosed is our check, made payable to the New Orleans Pro Bono Project, in the amount of $ ____________

Please respond by June 15, 1995 to ensure listing on invitation.

New Orleans Pro Bono Project
601 St. Charles Avenue • New Orleans, LA 70130
581-4043

CORPORATE SOLICITATION

April 7, 1995

1~

Re: JUSTICE FOR ALL BALL, September 8, 1995

Dear 2~:

The New Orleans Pro Bono Project's plans are under way for its annual fundraising event, The Justice for All Ball. This year's Ball will take place on September 8, 1995, once again at historic Gallier Hall with New Orleans' finest restaurants donating gourmet food and beverages.

The Justice for All Ball, which will be in its seventh year, is a premier event in the legal community. Hundreds of judges, lawyers, and private citizens come together for the evening to support this essential program. Support from you and others in the local business community have made this possible.

As you know, the Pro Bono Project is a non-profit organization comprised of lawyers volunteering to represent indigent clients in civil matters. While the volunteer attorneys donate their time, the Pro Bono Project still requires funds for administration of the hundreds of cases that are handled every year. It is only with the generosity and support of firms such as yours that the Pro Bono Project will be able to carry on its work.

Because of my belief that pro bono work is essential to this community, I have agreed to serve as the 1995 Chair of the event. I hope you will join me in helping to provide legal services to those in distress.

Each Patron and Sponsor will be listed in our mailing to over 7,000 attorneys and companies in the Greater New Orleans area. Please return the enclosed reply and your contribution by May 1, 1995 to assure your listing.

Should you have any questions about the Pro Bono Project or the Justice for All Ball, you may also call Harry Rosenberg, Chair of the Board of Directors (584-9219), or Rachel Paisant, the Executive Director of the Pro Bono Project (581-4043).

Thanking you in advance for your consideration and support, and with warm regards, I remain,

Sincerely,

Larry Lundy
Honorary Chairperson

Enclosure

RESTAURANT SOLICITATION LETTER

1~

Re: The Justice For All Ball
September 8, 1995

Dear 2~

In 1986, the New Orleans Pro Bono Project was established by the Louisiana Bar Foundation to provide free legal assistance to indigent clients in our community. The Project is a volunteer lawyer program where members of the Greater New Orleans area bar are asked to volunteer their legal services in civil matters.

While our volunteer attorneys donate their time, the Project still requires funds for administration of the hundreds of cases that are handled on an annual basis. It is necessary that we make a direct appeal to our local community in an effort to raise money.

We have invited several New Orleans area restaurants to participate in this black-tie optional event by donating specialty dishes of which they are particularly proud. All participating restaurants will be recognized in our mailing to over 7000 attorneys in the metropolitan area. This target group represents an extremely committed, involved and successful segment of the local market, no doubt including many of your regular local customers.

This year we would like to recruit 3~ as a participating restaurant for the Ball scheduled for Friday, September 8, 1995, to be held once again at Gallier Hall. We hope that you will join in supporting this worthwhile event. Please call Rachel Paisant, our Executive Director at 581-4043 or me at 566-1311 at your earliest convenience to confirm your participation.

With kindest regards and thanking you in advance for your support, I am

Sincerely,

Harry Rosenberg
Chairman

HR\mh

SENT TO NEWSPAPERS, RADIO AND TELEVISION STATIONS

June 30, 1994

For immediate release:

PRO BONO PROJECT TO RAISE MONEY TO PROVIDE FREE LEGAL SERVICES FOR THE INDIGENT

The New Orleans Pro Bono Project, a volunteer lawyer program is mobilizing the community to help provide free civil legal services to the indigent in the greater New Orleans area.

The Sixth **Annual Justice For All Ball** will be held Friday, September 9, 1994 at Gallier Hall from 8:00 p.m. to midnight. Famous New Orleans restaurants are donating specialty dishes for the event. There will be music and dancing to Charmaine Neville.

A special raffle consisting of items valued from $100 to $950 will be an additional feature. Local artists and businesses have donated items for this feature. Raffle tickets can be purchased in advance as well as the night of the Ball at $5/per chance or six chances for $25.00. Winner need not be present. All raffle proceeds will augment the New Orleans Pro Bono Project's fundraising efforts.

The New Orleans Pro Bono Project relies upon attorneys who volunteer their time to deliver legal services, but funding to administer the program is crucial. A recent study of the legal problems of the poor in Greater New Orleans found that the gap between need and available legal services is greater in this city than elsewhere in the nation. One out of every three people in New Orleans meets the federal poverty level and is unable to afford legal services. The New Orleans Pro Bono Project affords these people the opportunity to access the system of justice in civil matters.

"The **Justice For All Ball** will help insure that we come closer to the ideal of justice for all in New Orleans," Pro Bono Project Board Chair Thomas A. Casey, Jr. said. The New Orleans Pro Bono Project was established by the Louisiana Bar Foundation in 1986. Approximately 1,000 attorneys volunteer their time to offer free legal assistance to the poor through the program.

Tickets to the **Justice For All Ball** are $75.00 per person. Complimentary parking is provided.

Tickets may be obtained by calling (504) 581-4043. For further information, contact Rachel Paisant at the above number.

REMINDER

The yearly "Justice for All Ball", which is the New Orleans Pro Bono Project's major fundraiser, will be held on Friday, September 9, 1994 at 8:00 p.m. at Gallier Hall. Those of you who have attended in the past know that it has developed into one of the premiere fundraisers in New Orleans, and is attended by close to 1,000 lawyers, judges and their guests. Also, at $75 per person ($50 for lawyers practicing less than five years), it is reasonably priced. Obviously, the proceeds of the event go to a great cause -- the provision of free legal services for needy residents in this area. For information about tickets, call 581-4043.

JUSTICE FOR ALL BALL
September 8, 1995

TIME LINE OF PLANNING FOR EVENT

January	Ball Committee named
February	Initial meeting with committee members Create various solicitation lists: Master restaurant list Master corporate solicitation list Confirm Honorary Chairman Have pledge cards printed to insert with solicitation letters Confirm location - downpayment to reserve Hall Decide on format of event
March	Committee meeting Begin solicitations of restaurants and corporate sponsors - sample letters in packet (the sooner the better) Recruit caterer Work on invitation design: recruit artist, graphic co. to design invitation.
April	Have committee begin follow up work with restaurants and corporations assigned by letter or phone calls. Confirm entertainment
May	Committee meeting Continue solicitation follow up by committee Confirm invitation design Identify printer- have found printers unwilling to donate their services - Bid job out. (this is one of your most expensive costs) Confirm caterer. In recent years, we have gone with a Hotel that does outside catering. Since they already have the equipment and staff onhand, this eliminates the additional contractors and costs.
June	Committee meeting Continue solicitation follow up by committee Confirm printer - obtain final deadline from printer

July	Committee meeting Final printing deadline usually 2-3 weeks before mailing date Finalize contributor listings Obtain mailing labels - bar association donates Turn final list of restaurants over to the caterer-Caterer then surveys vendors needs and makes final arrangments Finalize decorations. Letter from the Chief Judicial Administrator goes out to all the judges encouraging their attendance.
August	Mass mailout of invitations - August 1, 1995 Press releases are sent 3 weeks prior to the event. Follow up phone calls are made the week before. Patron/Sponsors tickets are mailed out. Individual tickets are mailed as soon as RSVP's and monies are received. Publicity flyers are sent to law firms, courts, law schools, bar association offices ... Postcards with the inivitation design are mailed either 2 wks. before or 2 wks after invitations are mailed to targeted lists. Gifts if any are sent to Patrons Make sure have all gifts certificates and items for raffle. Finalize all arrangements. Recruit volunteers to help with door, raffle, etc. Make a final to-do list for the night of the Ball
September	Complete volunteer and staff assignments Contact and confirm attendance of those who will be in photos for the newspaper. **D-Day September 8, 1995** Final committee meeting - debriefing Follow up with thanks you to all contributors. Follow up with press with results of the event. **Rest!**

TRAINING

The Teaching Clinic: A Model for Training Volunteer Attorneys

by Alice Bussiere and Mary Viviano

The Volunteer Legal Services Program of the Bar Association of San Francisco (VLSP), winner of the American Bar Association's 1985 Harrison Tweed Award, has an innovative recruitment and training program that meets the needs of the clients, the volunteer attorneys, and the private attorney involvement project.

The VLSP training model, known as the teaching clinic, is based on a simple but effective concept that can be adapted easily to other private attorney involvement programs. It combines elements of a law school clinical program and a neighborhood legal services office to ensure that the volunteer attorneys have the information and support they need and to match attorneys with clients for quick and efficient delivery of services. Because of client demand and attorney interest, the first VLSP training clinic was created for family law cases. However, the design has been adapted for guardianship cases in cooperation with the National Center for Youth Law, and a landlord-tenant clinic is now underway.

The Teaching Clinic

The process starts at the VLSP office. A staff paralegal screens potential clients for eligibility and takes down pertinent information about the client's situation. Those cases that cannot be resolved with the advice of a VLSP staff attorney are accepted for the next clinic or assignment to a current VLSP panel attorney.

VLSP staff meet regularly to decide which cases are most appropriate for the clinic. Director Tanya Neiman stresses that VLSP does not place only the easy or uncontested cases in the clinic: "We are looking for cases that will provide a good learning experience for volunteer attorneys, and the teaching clinic allows us to place contested cases with confidence."

The clients assigned to the clinic are given an appointment for the next scheduled session. The appointments are made to allow volunteer attorneys about two hours of training before they meet with their clients.

On the evening of the clinic, the volunteer attorneys meet with two experienced attorneys who are experts in the substantive area of the law and members of the VLSP staff. There are usually six to eight volunteer attorneys at each clinic; sessions are held at Hastings Law School or at the offices of participating law firms or corporations. At the clinic, the volunteer attorneys receive written practice materials, which include an outline of the law and copies of relevant forms. VLSP develops the written materials in cooperation with private attorneys and local legal services programs according to the expertise available. For example, the National Center for Youth Law compiled information for the guardianship manual, while private attorneys undertook the major responsibility for writing the family law materials.

During the first part of the clinic, the expert attorneys provide an overview of substantive and procedural issues. These "mini lectures" include comments on local practice, instruction in the use of basic forms, and other practical advice on handling individual cases.

Next, the group as a whole engages in a roundtable discussion of the cases awaiting assignment that evening. The VLSP staff person presents the cases and provides pertinent details as the expert attorneys discuss how to handle each situation. The experts identify what steps the attorney should take and what additional facts are needed. This discussion helps the attorney who will accept the case to prepare for the initial interview and to develop a strategy for representing the client. It also gives the volunteers some sense of the complexity of each situation and the time that will be involved in each case so that they can accept cases that will be appropriate to their interests and to their schedules. At the same time, the discus-

---

Alice Bussiere is a staff attorney at the National Center for Youth Law, 1663 Mission St., 5th Fl., San Francisco, CA 94103, (415) 543-3307. Mary Viviano is the director of the Public Interest Clearinghouse in San Francisco, 198 McAllister, San Francisco, CA 94102, (415) 557-4014. The Volunteer Legal Services Program of the Bar Association of San Francisco is located at 220 Bush St., San Francisco, CA 94104, (415) 392-3960.

sions provide all of the volunteers information on a variety of issues and ways of approaching cases. This information will be useful to them in other pro bono cases and in their private practice as well.

After the general discussion, the cases are assigned, and the attorneys meet with the clients who have been given appointments for that evening. The expert attorneys remain available for consultation during and after the interviews so that volunteer attorneys can get information or advice immediately. In some cases, expert attorneys have helped the volunteers prepare forms or advice for the client the same day.

For future questions, the experts remain available for telephone consultation. In addition, volunteer lawyers have access to free training videotapes designed for less experienced attorneys and to VLSP staff who can answer questions or will locate an experienced attorney who can provide additional assistance if necessary. The clinic class members also provide a support group in that volunteer attorneys can turn to each other to talk over legal issues, ethical questions or other problems that arise in the attorney-client relationship.

Once a clinic panel has been trained, the volunteer attorneys continue to accept new cases in that area of the law as needed. VLSP conducts additional clinics according to the client demand and the attorneys' needs. For example, VLSP schedules regular family law clinics to provide a constant pool of attorneys for these cases. However, the guardianship clinic was conducted once in the past year and will be repeated only when the current panel of attorneys can no longer handle the incoming requests. VLSP holds centrally located clinics at convenient times for attorneys recruited individually and conducts special clinics at large law firms or corporations where several attorneys indicate an interest in participating. Recently, VLSP conducted a clinic at the headquarters for the Bank of America.

The Program's Success

The VLSP training program is a success from many perspectives. The clinic design ensures that clients will see an attorney as quickly as possible and will receive efficient and effective services. The combination of written materials, oral presentation and consultative support gives the volunteer attorneys the best possible preparation for their cases. This preparation is particularly important for programs like VLSP that rely heavily on new admittees and corporate counsel who are not always familiar with the issues faced by low-income clients.

The preparation and support provide a good experience for volunteer attorneys who could be easily frustrated if they were left to fend for themselves in an unfamiliar area of law. The combination of practical experience and training provides an excellent start for the new lawyer and is useful to more experienced practitioners who wish to expand their business into other areas of the law.

The teaching clinic is an effective recruitment tool that draws lawyers who are willing to take on pro bono cases in exchange for training and practical experience. VLSP takes advantage of this attraction for new admittees by stepping up its recruitment at bar admission time. VLSP staff provides information at the swearing-in ceremonies for new lawyers and by mail to new admittees. The local legal newspaper, *The Recorder*, also runs a news item describing the program at that time.

Tanya Neiman reports that the clinic is equally helpful in recruiting corporate attorneys. Lawyers who would otherwise be reluctant to handle cases outside of their area of expertise are willing to undertake pro bono cases if they are assured of the help and support they need.

At the same time, the clinic helps to retain attorneys. Those who no longer have time to devote to ongoing cases or who are "burned out" can serve as trainers or consultants and can help prepare and update materials. This gives experienced attorneys a chance to participate in pro bono activities without becoming overwhelmed by cases and provides a much needed change of pace.

Conclusion

Training is an important component of every successful private bar involvement project. A good training program will help to ensure that clients receive high-quality legal services, will provide the volunteer attorneys with a good learning experience, and will promote recruitment and retention of volunteer attorneys. The VLSP teaching clinic meets these goals. In addition, according to Tanya Neiman, "Everybody loves it. Everybody has a good time."

FAMILY LAW for the PRO BONO ATTORNEY

Sponsored by the Virginia State Bar

April 23, 1992
Richmond Omni Hotel

Craig M. Burshem
Virginia Poverty Law Center

These materials were reprinted with permission of the Bar Association of the City of Richmond and Central Virginia Legal Aid Society.

This program was financially assisted through the Continuing Legal Education Grant Fund Program of the Virginia Law Foundation.

LECTURE OUTLINE

I. Overview of the materials.
   A. Overview of Divorce, Spousal Support and Equitable Distribution.
   B. Contested Custody: The Law and Practice.
   C. Child Support and the Division of Child Support Enforcement.
   D. Juvenile Court Practice and Forms.

II. Additional Resources.
   A. Family Law & Practice - The Virginia Law Foundation.
   B. Virginia Domestic Relations Handbook - Margaret Brinig.
   C. Virginia Lawyer.
   D. Local Pro bono coordinator and legal aid attorneys.

III. Types of Pro Bono cases.
   A. Uncontested divorces.
   B. Contested divorces.
   C. Custody hearings in the JDR court.
   D. Adoptions.
   E. Name changes.

IV. The Client Interview.

V. The Divorce Case.
   A. Bill of Complaint.
      1. Jurisdiction.
      2. Venue.
      3. Ground.
   B. Pendente Lite hearing.
      1. Support.
      2. Other relief.
   C. Separation agreement.

VI. Contested Custody: The Law and Practice.

   A. Jurisdictional Issues.
      1. Juvenile and domestic relations court or the circuit court.
         a. JDR custody/visitation hearing.
         b. Circuit Court *pendente lite* hearing.
      2. Jurisdiction between states.
         a. Federal parental kidnapping protection act.
         b. Uniform child custody jurisdiction act.

1. Best interest of the child.
2. Absence of *Res Judicata.*
3. Natural parent preference.
4. Factors to consider in custody determination.
5. Custody dispute between parents.
6. Natural parent versus a third party.
7. Change in custody.

C. Change in custody.
D. Appeal from juvenile and domestic relations court.
E. Visitation.
   1. Reasonable visitation.
   2. Specified visitation.
   3. Visitation of more than 110 days.
   4. Custodial parent changing residence.
   5. Sexual abuse.
F. Practical Considerations.

VII. What is the State IV-D Program?

A. 1975 - Establishment of Part IV-D of the Social Security Act.
B. 1984 amendments to the Act.
C. Services provided by the IV-D system.
   1. Locating absent parents.
   2. Establishing paternity.
   3. Establishing support orders.
   4. Modifying support orders.
   5. Enforcing support orders.
D. ADC and the divorce decree.

VIII. Juvenile Court Practice and Forms.

A. Statutory guidelines.
   1. Calculation of support.
   2. Cost added to obligation.
   3. Factors used to deviate.

Craig M. Burshem
Virginia Poverty Law Center
9 West Main Street
Richmond, VA 23220

PRO BONO HOUSING LAW

Cosponsored by

THE BAR ASSOCIATION OF THE CITY OF RICHMOND

and

CENTRAL VIRGINIA LEGAL AID SOCIETY, INC.

Dates of Training: October 23,
October 30, November 6, 1990

Location: Hunton & Williams
707 East Main Street
Richmond, Virginia

SCHEDULE

Tuesday, October 23, 1990

5:15 p.m. --	Opening Remarks	Lonnie D. Nunley
5:25 p.m. --	Introduction of The Honorable John D. Butzner, Jr.	John C. Kenny
5:35 p.m. --	Remarks	The Honorable John D. Butzner, Jr.
5:45 p.m. --	Private Sector Residential Landlord-Tenant Law	Frank A. Porter
8:00 p.m. --	Coffee Break	
8:15 p.m. --	State Procedure In Housing Law	Marilynn C. Goss
8:45 p.m. --	Regulatory, Ethical, And Policy Issues In Pro Bono Housing Law	Henry W. McLaughlin

SCHEDULE

Tuesday, October 30, 1990

5:15 p.m. --	Opening remarks	John C. Kenny
5:25 p.m. --	Experiences from attorneys who were in the program during the last year	
6:00 p.m. --	Public Housing and Federal Housing Administration (F. H. A.) Subsidized Housing	Martin D. Wegbreit
8:00 p.m. --	Coffee Break	
8:15 p.m. --	Section 8 Housing	Martin D. Wegbreit

SCHEDULE

Tuesday, November 6, 1990

5:15 p.m. --	Opening Remarks	Robert L. Brooke
5:25 p.m. --	Housing Law: Perspectives from the Bench	The Honorable Walter W. Stout, III The Honorable E. L. Turlington, Jr. The Honorable William L. Wimbish
6:45 p.m. --	Representing The Tenant: Typical Problems and Responses	Henry Woodward
7:45 p.m. --	Coffee Break	
8:00 p.m. --	Representing The Tenant: Typical Problems and Responses (cont.)	Henry Woodward

1996 ABA PRO BONO PUBLICO

AWARDS

The American Bar Association
Standing Committee on Lawyers'
Public Service Responsibility
Invites Nominations for the
1996 ABA Pro Bono Publico Awards

Program Overview

The Standing Committee on Lawyers' Public Service Responsibility will present five awards to individual lawyers, law firms, government attorney offices, and corporate law departments that have demonstrated outstanding commitment to volunteer legal services for the poor and disadvantaged. The awards will be made at the Pro Bono Awards Assembly Luncheon in August 1996 at the ABA Annual Meeting in Orlando.

ROGRAM STATEMENT

he Pro Bono Publico Awards program seeks to identify and honor ndividual lawyers and small and large law firms, government ttorney offices, and corporate law departments that have enhanced he human dignity of others by improving or delivering volunteer egal services to our nation's poor or disadvantaged. These services re of critical importance to the increasing number of people in his country living in a state of poverty who are in need of legal epresentation to improve their lives.

here are lawyers whose contributions have made a difference in the ives of many. Their commitment, energy and new approaches to he delivery of pro bono service serve as models for others in the egal profession. Each nominator should describe fully the unique nd deserving efforts of the nominee.

andidates are legal professionals who commit their talent and raining to improve the quality of justice for those unable to afford lawyer. Some will be nominated for their longtime dedication to he delivery of pro bono legal services to the poor. Others, newer to he field, might be nominated for their creative approaches to the lelivery of volunteer legal services or their commitment to repreenting low-income persons. Some may have brought about egislation that contributes substantially to legal services to the poor.

AWARD CRITERIA

Individual attorneys who do not obtain their income delivering legal services to the poor are eligible. Large and small law firms, corporate law departments and government attorney offices whose members have collectively made an outstanding contribution fitting one of the award's criteria are also eligible.

Not more than five awardees will be selected from those who have excelled in one or more of the following ways:

(a) demonstrated dedication to the development and delivery of legal services to the poor through a pro bono program;

(b) contributed significant work toward developing innovative approaches to delivery of volunteer legal services;

(c) participated in an activity which resulted in satisfying previously unmet needs or in extending services to underserved segments of the population;

(d) successfully litigated pro bono cases that favorably affected the provision of other services to the poor;

(e) successfully achieved legislation that contributed substantially to legal services to the poor.

NOMINATION GUIDELINES

The Standing Committee urges nominators to choose only one worthy candidate a year. We understand that this may often be a difficult choice. If there is more than one worthy candidate in your community, separate nominations for each must be submitted.

To ensure the completeness of your nomination packet, you should include:

I. Nominee Information Sheet. The first page of the packet should be the nominee information sheet form in this brochure.

II. Candidate's Resume. The next two to three pages of the packet should be a resume or document which describes the candidate's background and other relevant activities. Information that would be helpful includes principal areas of practice, the number of years practicing law, other public service contributions, educational background, supporting documents and other bar association activities.

III. Nomination Narrative. Using as many pages as sary, explain how the candidate meets the criteria for Pro Bono Publico Award. Specify the nature of the pr bono contribution and identify those who have benef Whenever possible provide:

- specific documentation or other materials which demonstrate the candidate's pro bono contributio including articles, brochures and other documen tion; and
- no more than three names, telephone numbers a addresses of others who, if asked, could provide additional information.

IV. Letters of Support. You may include letters of su from other individuals and organizations that are aw the candidate's pro bono contribution.

Nominations and supporting materials should b 8-1/2 x 11 inch, 3 hole punched paper. Please s seven (7) copies of each nomination and suppor materials. Do not staple them in any way. A pape clip or removable binder clip will be sufficient.

SELECTION PROCESS

The Standing Committee on Lawyers' Public Service Responsibility will review the nominations in April, 1996 an select no more than five awardees. Award recipients will be fied no later than April 30, 1996. All Committee decisions w final and binding. The Committee reserves the right to awa fewer than five awards in order to protect the integrity of th awards program.

Nominations must be received by January 31, 199
No extensions will be granted.
Submit all materials to:
The Pro Bono Publico Awards-American Bar Associati
Division for Legal Services
Gwendolyn Y. Rowan
541 North Fairbanks Court, Chicago, Illinois 60611-3

Past Pro Bono Publico Award recipients include:

1995 Winners

Warren E. George
— San Francisco, California

Recognized for devoting extraordinary time to protecting the rights of California prisoners.

Amy Greer
— Pittsburgh, Pennsylvania

Recognized for her dedication and significant time devoted to providing a variety of pro bono legal services matters in her community.

David Schoen
— Montgomery, Alabama

Recognized for his enormous contribution to bringing about change in schools, prisons, jails, foster care, police departments, and election ballot access in the South.

Honorable William Van Nortwick, Jr.
—Jacksonville, Florida

Honored for his pivotal role in developing systems and policies to improve the provision of legal services to Florida's poor.

Jenner & Block
— Chicago, Illinois

Recognized for the firm's extensive pro bono commitment and team participation; each firm lawyer devoted more than 100 hours to providing pro bono legal services in each of the past two years.

1994 Winners

André Dennis
— Philadelphia, Pennsylvania

Honored for his dedicated pro bono representation of a member of the MOVE organization, his efforts to reshape the District Court's Prisoners' Civil Rights Panel of volunteer attorneys, and his representation of inmates in prisoners' rights cases.

Douglas Robinson
— Washington D.C.

Recognized for his dedication to ensuring that death

Award Background

The Pro Bono Publico Awards were established by the American Bar Association in 1984 to recognize lawyers and law firms for extraordinarily noteworthy contributions to extending legal services to the poor and disadvantaged. The recipients exemplify the volunteer tradition of the legal profession. The program is administered by the Association's Standing Committee on Lawyers' Public Service Responsibility.

Steel Hector & Davis
— Miami, Florida

Recognized for the firm's commitment and team participation in meeting the legal needs of the victims of Hurricane Andrew and for its leadership role in providing landlord/tenant representation through Dade County's "Put Something Back" program.

1993 Winners

Russell Austin
— Sacramento, California

Recognized for his efforts which resulted in significant expansion of the level of financial support for the Voluntary Legal Services Program of Northern California.

Oliver Hill
—Richmond, Virginia

Chosen for his dedication to eliminating segregation, Mr. Hill filed numerous landmark cases which established rights for minorities.

Edward Kelaher
— Surfside Beach, South Carolina

1992 Winners

Joseph S. Genova
— New York, New York

Chosen for his leadership in documenting the need for free legal services in New York and spearheading the state bar association's role in the expansion of pro bono.

Robert E. Juceam
— New York, New York

Honored for his extraordinary efforts to ensure that Haitian refugees receive fair and equal treatment from the United States government.

Suzanne E. Turner
— Philadelphia, Pennsylvania

Selected for her direct involvement in creating a framework within which pro bono efforts were brought into the mainstream of a large firm practice and in increasing pro bono service in her community.

Douglas Young
— San Francisco, California

Honored for his dedication and extraordinary time, energy and personal resources devoted to the representation of indigent persons, most notably two persons appealing death sentences.

Nelson, Mullins, Riley & Scarborough
— Columbia, South Carolina

Recognized for creating a model internal pro bono program in which over 75 percent of the attorneys and many support staff participate, and which provided service in matters ranging from death penalty appeals to housing, health care, handicapped children, and the First Amendment.

1991 Winners

Manlin M. Chee
— Greensboro, North Carolina

Honored for her extraordinary work on the behalf of aliens, calling them "the most oppressed of our indigent population."

Edmond M. Connor
— Irvine, California

Recognized for his

m. Reece Smith, Jr.
— Tampa, Florida

lected for dedicating more than 40 years to advocating pro no activities and urging creative partnerships between the ate bar and the legal services community.

lston, Rutherford, Tardy & Van Slyke
— Jackson, Mississippi

ixteen-member law firm honored for accepting a minimum 100 pro bono cases a year and for its efforts to raise the statu- limitation for court appointed criminal defense attorneys.

Victor Marerro
— New York, New York

Recognized for his leadership in assessing resources and legal needs of the poor in New York and his efforts to create new means of representing the underprivileged.

Covington and Burling
— Washington, D.C.

Selected for its extraordinary commitment to public service, the firm's pro bono representation consistently accounts for about 8-10% of the firm's total billable hours.

— Dayton, Ohio

Recognized for his leadership in the development of the Greater Dayton Volunteer Lawyers Project.

Amitai Schwartz
— San Francisco, California

Selected for his unparalleled dedication to expanding the delive legal services to indigent clients in San Francisco.

Hogan & Hartson
— Washington, D.C.

Honored for the firm's more than twenty year commitment to handling pro bono cases through its unique public service departı

American Bar Association 1996 Pro Bono Publico Awards

ominee Information Sheet
ease type or print all information legibly)

ominee's Name ______________________________

lress ______________________________

/State/Zip ______________________________

ephone ( ) ______________________________

ominator's Name ______________________________

ress ______________________________

State/Zip ______________________________

ephone ( ) ______________________________

bmit to:
erican Bar Association
Pro Bono Publico Awards
ssion for Legal Services
endolyn Y. Rowan
1 N. Fairbanks Court
ago, Illinois 60611-3314

Nomination Deadline: Postmarked by January 31, 1996

No extensions will be granted.

Please circle the criteria that appl

Nominee has:

(a) demonstrated dedication to the development and delive of legal services to the poor through a pro bono progran

(b) contributed significant work toward developing innovativ approaches to delivery of volunteer legal services;

(c) participated in an activity which resulted in satisfying p ously unmet needs or in extending services to underserv segments of the population;

(d) successfully litigated pro bono cases that favorably affe the provision of other services to the poor;

(e) successfully achieved legislation that contributed substa tially to legal services to the poor.

Please attach information that documents what your nominee done to enhance the human dignity of others through improvi or delivering volunteer legal services to our nation's poor.

Nominations and supporting materials should be on 8-1/2 x 11 inch, 3 hole punched paper. Please send seven (7) copies of ea nomination and supporting materials. Do not staple them in any way. A paper clip or removable binder clip will be sufficient.

The San Diego Volunteer Lawyer Program

cordially invites you to

The 1995 Justice For All Awards Dinner

Honoring the volunteers, law firms, sponsors and contributors whose participation and support provide pro bono legal services to San Diego's poor.

With special recognition to our award recipients:

PRO BONO ATTORNEY OF THE YEAR

PRO BONO LAW FIRM OF THE YEAR

COMMUNITY SERVICE AWARD

Keynote Speaker:

Barbara Boxer

United States Senator from
the State of California

Friday, June 2, 1995

Sheraton Harbor Island Hotel East
Harbor Island Ballroom

5:30 p.m. No-Host Reception.
7:00 p.m. Dinner and Program
Business Attire

The 1995 Justice For All Awards Dinner

Name ______________________________

Firm ______________________________

Address ______________________________

City/State/Zip ______________________________

Phone Voice ________________ Facsimile ________________

Please reserve:

________ Patron Table(s) at $1,500.00 for table of 10.

Please seat me/us with ______________________________

________ Individual Ticket(s) at $100.00 each.

________ I cannot attend, but wish to support SDVLP with a contribution of $ ________________

Seating is limited and reservations will be accepted on a first-come basis. Reservations must be received by May 26, 1995. No cancellations or refunds. Your contributions in excess of $40.00 per person may be tax deductible. Please enclose checks payable to SDVLP, 225 Broadway, Suite #800, San Diego, CA 92101. Tickets will be held at the door.

THE 1995 JUSTICE FOR ALL AWARDS DINNER

SHERATON HARBOR ISLAND EAST HOTEL
HARBOR ISLAND BALLROOM

June 2, 1995

The San Diego Volunteer Lawyer Program welcomes you to the Seventh Annual Justice for All Awards Dinner. This is a special night for the SDVLP Board of Directors and staff, because it is dedicated to recognizing and thanking all of our volunteers, sponsors, contributors and supporters.

Because of the generous pro bono work of our volunteers and the contributions of law firms, philanthropic groups, foundations and individuals, SDVLP provided legal services to more than 12,000 needy clients in 1994. More than 60,000 hours of legal assistance were donated to victims of domestic violence, dependent and abused children, persons living with AIDS and HIV infection, the homeless and disabled, refugees and immigrants and other individuals and charitable organizations.

We congratulate and thank all who have contributed to the continued success of the program. We are especially grateful to those who are being honored tonight. We invite all of you to an evening of celebration and renewed dedication to serving the community and making equal access to justice a reality.

1995 JUSTICE FOR ALL AWARDS DINNER COMMITTEE

Candace M. Carroll
Stephen F. Yunker
Co-Chairs

Policy and Program	Hon. Maria T. Arroyo-Tabin
	Carl R. Poirot
Table Sales	Candace M. Carroll, Chair
	Peter H. Benzian
	James E. Chodzko
	Timothy D. Cohelan
	Craig D. Higgs
	Joyce A. McCoy
	James F. Stiven
Underwriting	Robert Scott Dreher, Co-Chair
	Debra K. Maurer, Co-Chair
	Jane Alshuler
	Cynthia H. Cwik
	Jay W. Jeffcoat
	Janis K. Stocks
	Timothy B. Taylor
	Stephen F. Yunker
Phonathon	Vincent J. Axelson
	Timothy B. Taylor
Hotel/Administration	Pam Pressler Sullivan
	Cheryl A. Martinez
Drawing	Drue A. Koons
	Solveig Deuprey

Video Production Compliments of John Morris, Esq.

PROGRAM

WELCOME AND INTRODUCTIONS
Candace M. Carroll
Stephen F. Yunker

SPECIAL GUEST
Donald R. Fischbach
California State Bar President

KEYNOTE SPEAKER
Barbara Boxer
U.S. Senator
State of California

MOMENT OF REMEMBRANCE
Jay W. Jeffcoat
Gray Cary Ware & Freidenrich

RECOGNITION FOR OUTSTANDING SERVICE
Hon. Maria T. Arroyo-Tabin

Presenter Carl R. Poirot
San Diego Volunteer Lawyer Program

PRESENTATION OF AWARDS

Jane Alshuler
Bar Association of Northern San Diego County

COMMUNITY SERVICE AWARD FINALISTS
Cynthia D. Baker
Fernando Rhine Magallanes
Steven Sweat

Presenter Dale B. Walls
Legal Aid Society of San Diego

PRO BONO LAW FIRM OF THE YEAR FINALISTS
Brobeck, Phleger & Harrison
Laturno & Graves
Sheppard, Mullin, Richter & Hampton

Presenter Regina A. Petty
San Diego County Bar Association

PRO BONO ATTORNEY OF THE YEAR FINALISTS
Allen R. Cocumelli
Ann M. Durst
Joseph F. Oberle

Presenter Cynthia A. Bashant
Lawyers Club of San Diego

CLOSING
Stephen F. Yunker

SECTION 4

SECTION 4: CREATION/ADMINISTRATION OF BAR-SPONSORED PRO BONO PROGRAMS

This section of the handbook deals with bar associations' direct operation and management of pro bono programs through state support programs, direct delivery of pro bono legal services and public legal education.

State Support Programs

Discussion

Many state bar associations have enacted a statewide pro bono plan and program that provides statewide support for pro bono activities. State support programs exist in states that have statewide direct pro bono delivery programs, as well as in states that do not. A primary objective of a statewide pro bono plan and program should be to promote and coordinate statewide planning.

Some bar associations administer a statewide pro bono support program within the structure of the bar itself. Others create an independent 501(c)(3) for that purpose. In either event, the program should be adequately staffed. Some bar associations employ a pro bono support director. Because of their access to the statewide bar network, state support directors can be instrumental in raising the level of pro bono activity on a statewide basis. The state support director often works with bar committees and other statewide entities involved in the effort to deliver pro bono legal services to persons of limited means. State pro bono support directors also should work with legal services organizations in the state to implement integrated strategies for addressing unmet legal needs.

In addition, state support directors work with state bar leaders on a wide range of issues, including pro bono resolutions, statewide activation plans for the delivery of pro bono services, planning state bar pro bono awards ceremonies, and coordinating statewide pro bono conferences. They also may handle the bulk of the administrative work for state bar committees that are evaluating options for increasing the availability of legal services, including fundraising initiatives, attorney reporting of pro bono work, and innovative delivery models.

State support directors also serve as a tremendous resource to local bar associations, particularly those in small communities where there is little organized pro bono activity. The state support director can provide technical assistance to local bar associations, including assistance with the activation of local pro bono plans, training volunteer lawyers, and providing written materials related to the delivery of pro bono services.

Pros

- ☞ State support programs enhance the level of pro bono activity on a statewide basis.
- ☞ State support programs facilitate statewide planning of integrated strategies for addressing unmet legal needs of persons of limited means.
- ☞ State support programs provide staff resources to bar committees addressing pro bono matters.
- ☞ State support programs provide technical assistance to local bar associations.

Cons

- ☞ State support programs may require the hiring of paid staff.
- ☞ State support programs may be administratively intensive.
- ☞ State support programs may conflict with local bar efforts.

Contacts

State Bar of California, Office of Legal Services
Staff Contacts: Eve Hershcopf (415) 561-8213 and Sharon Ngim (415) 561-8267, Pro Bono Program Developers
Volunteer Contact: Jack Londen (415) 677-7415

Texas Lawyers Care
Staff Contact: Julie Oliver, Executive Director (512) 463-1463 x 2155
Volunteer Contact: Kirk Watson (512) 476-4346

State Bar of Wisconsin
Staff Contact: Deborah Tobin, Pro Bono Program Director (608) 257-3838 x 6177
Volunteer Contact: John Skilton (608) 258-4229

People's Pro Bono Action Center, Inc. (Maryland)
Staff Contact: Sharon Goldsmith, Executive Director (410) 837-9379
Volunteer Contact: Lee A. Caplin (301) 759-1000

Examples

People's Pro Bono Action Center, Inc. (Maryland) Program Description (Attachment 4-A)

Texas Lawyers Care Program Description (Attachment 4-B)

Direct Delivery Programs

Discussion

A number of state and local bar associations operate programs that provide direct delivery of legal services to persons of limited means through pro bono attorneys. In determining whether to undertake a direct delivery program, bar associations should carefully assess the availability of legal services to persons of limited means through existing programs. Bar associations are encouraged to collaborate with other legal services providers in the community to determine whether an additional direct delivery program is the most efficient and cost-effective mechanism for enhancing access to the legal system for persons of limited means. Direct delivery programs are a tremendous undertaking, and bar associations should not attempt to administer them unless they are prepared to accept the administrative and financial responsibility involved. Bar associations considering the administration of a direct delivery system should consult the ABA *Standards For Programs Providing Civil Pro Bono Legal Services To Persons Of Limited Means*.

The structure of direct delivery programs varies widely. In some communities, a bar-sponsored pro bono program works closely with the legal services organization in administering the direct delivery program. Some pro bono projects are jointly sponsored by the bar and the legal services organization, and in some cases, the entire program is jointly sponsored or funded. Other legal services organizations subcontract their private attorney involvement (PAI) component to bar associations. In some communities, the bar-sponsored pro bono program is completely independent of the legal services program. Finally, some direct delivery programs are structured as independent 501(c)(3) corporations with bar sponsorship or support. Bar associations should carefully consider these options before determining the organizational structure of the direct delivery system.

Direct delivery programs take on many different forms. Several forms of direct delivery are discussed below.

Intake and Referral Systems

Discussion

The most common form of direct delivery of legal services by pro bono programs is through client intake, referral, or a combination of both. Intake and referral systems may be local or statewide. Statewide programs can provide for allocation of pro bono resources to areas of the state where there is little or no organized pro bono activity.

Intake and referral systems generally combine the resources of both paid staff and volunteers. Some programs handle client intake as well as the referral of cases to volunteer lawyers. In these programs, volunteers or staff (either lawyers or nonlawyers) do the initial screening of clients for income eligibility and the nature of their legal problem. This screening can take place on the telephone or in-person. An increasing number of programs are using telephone "hotlines" to handle initial client intake and render brief advice. Following the initial intake, some clients may be interviewed more extensively by volunteer or staff attorneys. Certain clients are then referred to volunteer attorneys for representation.

Other programs handle only the referral of cases to volunteer attorneys. These programs receive cases from legal services programs or other organizations after the initial client intake is conducted. The referral entity then matches clients with volunteer attorneys on the referral panel. In either scenario, the program should maintain some oversight over referred cases. A number of operational systems and procedures must be in place before an intake and referral program is implemented, including: determination of income-eligibility standards and case priorities; recruitment and training of volunteers; methods for handling conflicts of interest; procedures for tracking matters; malpractice insurance for volunteers; and grievance procedures for clients.

Intake and referral systems offer attorneys many volunteer opportunities. Individual attorneys can volunteer to conduct in-person intake, staff screening hotlines, accept referrals, or mentor other pro bono attorneys in specified areas of legal expertise. In addition, law firms, government offices, bar sections, and corporate counsel offices can participate by handling certain aspects of an intake and referral system. For example, attorneys from a particular corporate counsel office may conduct intake on certain days or nights each month; a law firm can accept multiple referrals in specified subject areas; the family law section can provide mentoring to less-experienced pro bono attorneys handling domestic cases; and the tax or business law section may represent not-for-profit organizations that benefit persons of limited means.

Pros

- ☞ Direct delivery through intake and referral systems enables bar associations to exercise more control over the delivery of legal services.

- ☞ Direct delivery through intake and referral systems demonstrates the bar association's clear commitment to pro bono service.
- ☞ Statewide intake and referral programs can provide for allocation of pro bono resources to areas of the state where there is little or no organized pro bono activity.
- ☞ Intake and referral systems provides multiple options for attorneys wishing to provide pro bono services.

Cons

- ☞ Intake and referral programs are administratively intensive.
- ☞ Intake and referral programs require the expenditure of financial resources to hire staff and pay for office space, equipment, etc.
- ☞ Intake and delivery systems may duplicate or conflict with other existing efforts.

Contacts

Mississippi Volunteer Lawyers Project
Staff Contact: Phyllis Thornton, Director (601) 948-4471
Volunteer Contact: Ben J. Piazza, Jr. (601) 949-4796

State Bar of New Mexico "Lawyers Care" Project
Staff Contact: Alan Pannell, Project Coordinator (505) 843-8990
Volunteer Contact: Sarah Singleton (505) 986-2648

Idaho Volunteer Lawyers Project
Staff Contact: Carol Craighill (208) 334-4510
Volunteer Contact: Honorable Renae Hoff (208) 467-2171

Legal Aid Society of the Orange County Bar Association (Florida)
Staff Contact: Catherine Tucker, Executive Director (407) 841-8310
Volunteer Contact: Lawrence Matthews (407) 872-2200

Philadelphia Volunteers for the Indigent Program
Staff Contact: Margaret de Marteleire, Executive Director (215) 981-3787
Volunteer Contact: Jeffrey P. Bates (215) 587-0840

Examples

Description of Idaho Volunteer Lawyers Project (Attachment 4-C)

Job Description for Coordinator Position, State Bar of New Mexico "Lawyers Care" Project (Attachment 4-D)

Program Description, Philadelphia Volunteers for the Indigent Program (Attachment 4-E)

Description of Legal Aid Society of the Orange County Bar Association (Florida) (Attachment 4-F)

Clinics and Court-Based Projects

Discussion

Clinics are a tool for delivering legal advice and services to clients in a group setting. Because clinics serve clients through an alternative to the one-client/one-attorney model, they are a practical approach to dealing with legal matters for which the demand for pro bono and legal services attorneys outweighs the supply. Generally, one or more pro bono attorneys is matched with a group of clients in a clinic setting. In high-volume areas, such as family law, clinics often provide the most efficient way to utilize limited attorney resources. Clinics also are an excellent vehicle for training and using pro bono attorneys.

There are many different types of clinics, ranging from advice-only to full-service. A common model is the *pro se* advice-only clinic designed for unrepresented litigants. Advice clinics are effective tools for assisting clients who are handling their own divorces, particularly in cases where custody and property matters are not disputed by the parties. Advice clinics also are useful in advising clients about debtor-creditor matters and small claims proceedings.

Many advice clinics begin with a general presentation by a program staff member or a pro bono attorney about the law and procedures involved in the subject matter at hand. A videotape may be shown as part of this initial presentation. Subsequently, the staff and pro bono attorneys assist clients with the completion of forms and answer individual questions. Depending on the clinic format, clients may be scheduled for follow-up clinics as appropriate. Because advice clinics do not offer full representation to clients in their legal proceeding, clinic programs should include safeguards for referring clients to other resources when full legal representation is needed. In addition, bar programs sponsoring clinics should collaborate with other social services organizations to provide holistic delivery of services. Information relating to job training, family planning, housing, public benefits and health care can be presented along with legal advice.

The clinic approach also can be used in the intake process, as an aspect of a full-service delivery program. Clients with specific legal problems, such as debtor-creditor matters, are scheduled to meet with volunteer attorneys in a clinic setting. Volunteer attorneys address the clients as a group on general issues relating to the subject matter, and then meet individually with clients to discuss their particular situations. Clients who need additional representation after the initial intake session are referred to a pro bono attorney.

Some clinics operate in courthouses. Members of the judiciary and court administrator's staff tend to be very cooperative, and often will lend their support and resources to court-based projects. It is in their best interest to support efforts to address the legal needs of *pro se* litigants. Bar associations can work with the court system on other court-based projects as well. Some bar associations have initiated projects where pro bono attorneys are given a room in the courthouse to meet with *pro se* litigants and assist them with the completion of form pleadings. Other bar associations administer landlord-tenant projects, where pro bono attorneys routinely make themselves available to represent clients in landlord-tenant court. Finally, bar associations may provide pro bono attorneys to handle mediations referred by the court system.

Pros

- ☞ Clinics provide an efficient tool for handling high-volume areas of law.
- ☞ Clinics involve minimal costs.
- ☞ Clinics and court-based projects may utilize the resources of the court system.
- ☞ Clinics present opportunities for bar pro bono programs to collaborate with social services providers in an effort to provide holistic delivery of services.
- ☞ Clinics provide opportunities for volunteer attorneys who cannot provide full representation.

Cons

- ☞ Clinics can be labor-intensive.
- ☞ Clinics may provide less service to clients than is provided through representation by individual attorneys.
- ☞ There is a danger that pro se clinic clients may not follow through on their own, and therefore, the services may not be useful.

Contacts

Dade County "Put Something Back" Pro Bono Project (Florida)
Pro Se Divorce Clinic
Staff Contact: Sharon Langer, Executive Director (305) 579-5733

Volunteer Legal Services Project of Monroe County, Inc. (New York)
Debt Collection Advice Clinic
Staff Contact: Hanna Cohn, Executive Director (716) 232-3051
Volunteer Contact: Brian Zorn (716) 423-5900

Erie County Bar Association (New York)
Attorney of the Morning Project (Landlord-Tenant Matters)
Staff Contact: Robert Elardo, Managing Attorney, Volunteer Lawyers Project, Inc. (716) 847-0662

Volunteer Legal Services Program of the Bar Association of San Francisco
Staff Contact: Tanya Neiman, Executive Director (415) 267-0714
Volunteer Contact: Jack Londen (415) 677-7415

Examples

Description of Dade County "Put Something Back" Pro Bono Project Pro Se Divorce Clinic (Attachment 4-G)

Description of Volunteer Legal Services Project of Monroe County, New York Debt Collection Advice Clinic (Attachment 4-H)

Article in June, 1996 ABA Center for Pro Bono *Exchange*: "Court-Based Pro Bono" (Attachment 4-I)

Description of "One-Stop" Women's Clinic, Volunteer Legal Services Program of the Bar Association of San Francisco (Attachment 4-J)

Public Legal Education

Discussion

Public education about the law and the legal system is a relatively simple method through which bar associations can offer pro bono resources to persons of limited means. Public education often takes the form of speakers' bureaus, telephone hotlines, and publications (e.g. brochures and handbooks on specific legal matters). Generally, attorneys can be recruited fairly easily to participate in legal education activities. Public education provides an ideal option for attorneys who either are uncomfortable working with individual pro bono clients, or whose jobs preclude them from handling outside cases.

Through the bar association network and contacts with legal services organizations, bar members can identify low-income groups to be served by the speakers' bureau. These groups include churches, neighborhood groups, tenant groups, etc. Bar associations also can recruit pro bono attorneys to prepare written materials regarding legal matters that commonly impact persons of limited means. These materials can be made available to judges, clerk's offices, and legal services organizations, as well as distributed to public places in low-income communities. The preparation of written materials is often done in conjunction with clinics. Finally, pro bono attorneys can staff hotlines through which general legal information is provided to the public and, where appropriate, referrals are made to organizations providing legal services.

Pros

- ☞ Legal education programs usually are not very labor-intensive.
- ☞ Legal education projects provide pro bono opportunities for government attorneys and corporate counsel attorneys who may be prohibited from handling individual matters.

Cons

- ☞ Some costs may be associated with the publication of legal education materials and hotlines (particularly if toll-free numbers are used).

Contacts

The Virginia "Pro Bono Hotline" Project
Staff Contact: Henry W. McLaughlin III, Director, Central Virginia Legal Aid Society (804) 648-1012
Volunteer Contact: R. Terrence Ney (703) 712-5401

The State Bar of California, Office of Legal Services
Staff Contacts: Eve Hershcopf (415) 561-8213 and Sharon Ngim (415) 561-8267, Pro Bono Developers
Volunteer Contact: Jack Londen (415) 677-7415

Hennepin County Bar Association (Minnesota) Tel-Law Program
Staff Contact: Jane Schoeneke, Executive Director (612) 340-0022
Volunteer Contact: James L. Baillie (612) 347-7013

Mahoning County Bar Association (Ohio) Public Forums Project
Staff Contact: Georgia Murray (216) 746-1054

Examples

The State Bar of California Brochure on *How Do I Use the Small Claims Court?* (Attachment 4-K)

Project Description, The "Pro Bono Hotline," Sponsored by the Young Lawyers Section of the Virginia Bar Association and Central Virginia Legal Aid Society, Inc. (Attachment 4-L)

Description of the Hennepin County Bar Association (Minnesota) Tel-Law Program (Attachment 4-M)

SECTION 4 ATTACHMENTS

People's Pro Bono Action Center, Inc.

Ensuring Equal Access to Justice through Volunteerism

4A

MARYLAND
MARCH 1996

Today in Maryland ver 70 % of people ho need civil legal ervices aren't able to et or afford those ypes of services ..because they can not fford to hire an ttorney ...Lawyers lay a vital role in naking sure our ystem works for all ur people and pro ono is a critical part f that goal."

"Maryland lawyers have really stepped forward and are among the best in the nation as far as volunteering their time in order to help people get access to our system. The People's Pro Bono project was developed by Maryland awyers and to me that s the best answer to the problem."

The Honorable Benjamin L. Cardin

Increasing Lawyer Involvement

The mainstay of the pro bono effort are the lawyers who volunteer their time, expertise and compassion in assisting Maryland's indigent. Creating a greater awareness of pro bono service in the legal community and increasing the number of volunteer attorneys continues to be a primary focus of the Center.

Attorneys are most often drawn into pro bono work through active recruitment efforts. In addition to the referral of thousands of interested volunteers to provider organizations through the People's Pro Bono Campaign, the Center continuously places hundreds of volunteers a year with one of twenty-seven legal services programs throughout Maryland. Since the Campaign, Maryland has witnessed a 100% increase in the number of volunteer attorneys participating in an organized pro bono program.

Promotion and Recruitment

The People's Pro Bono Action Center utilizes a number of marketing techniques to recruit volunteers. They include:

- a regular column in the *Maryland State Bar Association's* (MSBA) *Bar Bulletin*
- articles in local and specialty bar publications, *The Daily Record*, *Afro-American*, and the *SunPaper* newspapers
- a special supplement in *The Daily Record* on pro bono activities
- distribution of materials and individual solicitations of new lawyers through admission ceremonies and presentations at the Professionalism Courses (new lawyers receive information about pro bono opportunities from the Action Center at least three times during their first year of practice)
- coordination of annual Pro Bono Opportunities Fairs for young lawyers (sponsored in conjunction with the MSBA Young Lawyers Section). This innovative program has earned awards from the MSBA and the American Bar Association (ABA) Commission on Partnership Programs, and was selected as a national model by the ABA Young Lawyer Affiliate Outreach Program. Over 120 volunteer referrals have been made from a single fair
- publication and distribution of the *Maryland Directory of Pro Bono Legal Services Programs and Opportunities* to approximately 500 law firms and over 5500 individuals
- targeted solicitations of

specialty bar associations, committees and sections

- institution of an annual pro bono reporting survey included in the Clients' Security Trust Fund mailing to 23,000 licensed practitioners with a solicitation for pro bono involvement
- presentations and exhibits at state, local and specialty bar conferences, meetings and special events
- initiation of meetings with law firm pro bono coordinators
- development of partnerships for marketing pro bono opportunities

All of the Action Center's promotional materials highlight the pressing and varied legal needs of the poor while introducing programs through which attorneys can make a critical difference in people's lives.

TRAINING

Training attorneys in substantive areas of the law in exchange for accepting pro bono cases has been effective in both recruiting and retaining volunteer attorneys, while assuring a level of quality representation. The Action Center sponsors a series of training programs and assists legal services providers educate volunteers in areas such as bankruptcy and consumer debt, domestic relations, disability, special education, employment discrimination, Child in Need of Assistance (CINA), and housing law. Other activities include regular publication of a statewide training calendar and the establishment and coordination

of the Maryland Institute for Continuing Professional Education of Lawyers (MICPEL)-Pro Bono Partnership Program subsidizing free or reduced fee seminars for pro bono attorneys.

INCLUSION OF NON-TRADITIONAL VOLUNTEERS

The Action Center has focused on expanding volunteer opportunities thereby engaging less traditional volunteers with particular emphasis on involving non-litigators such as transactional, tax and commercial lawyers, government attorneys, and law school faculty. These efforts include:

- designation of tax liaisons from the MSBA Section of Taxation to 14 different legal services organizations to act as counsel to the programs or their clients
- expansion of the Maryland Attorney General Office's Pro Bono Program by brokering new affiliations with legal services organizations and successfully urging the

"Amy is a lovable little girl who needed a mom and a dad and a stable home. We wanted to be her mom and dad. My husband works very hard but we could never have afforded to pursue Amy's adoption without Tom's legal services for free. She's a part of our family now. If we had not had a pro bono attorney, Amy would not be with us. It's that simple."

"...anytime I get involved with a pro bono program it's the kind of work that is personally enriching. I get a financial reward from my private practice. But more importantly I get an emotional reward for my pro bono work ... pro bono enhances the firm's image, improves the firm's morale and enriches the attorney's life."

Increasing Lawyer Involvement

acceptance of bankruptcy and other cases. Maryland's program is one of only five such programs in the country

- involvement of government lawyers, law school faculty and in-house corporate counsel in teaching basic legal education to English as a Second Language students through the Action Center's Legal Education and Access to Newcomers (LEAN) program
- establishment of an Attorney Emeritus Program enabling retired attorneys to engage in pro bono work by successfully urging the Standing Committee on Rules of Practice and Procedure to provide an exception to Rule 1-312 (maintaining an office for the practice of law)
- presentations to faculty members of both University of Maryland and University of Baltimore Schools of Law and matching them with legal services providers

Support for Pro Bono Attorneys

The Action Center routinely responds to inquiries from lawyers about pro bono opportunities or their volunteer work. The Action Center continuously seeks to identify mechanisms for simplifying and supporting the work of pro bono attorneys. An increased need for bankruptcy attorneys prompted the Action Center to arrange for a special expedited admission process for pro bono lawyers not yet admitted to the federal bar.

The Action Center has arranged for other donated support services from court reporters, investigators and paralegals. Each year, the Center negotiates free LEXIS/NEXIS computer research time. It also collaborated on and provided financial support to produce the *Pro Bono Desk Manual*, a resource tool for volunteers on substantive legal issues relevant to low-income clients.

RECOGNITION

The Action Center has recognized the contributions of the legal community through awards, special events and the media including:

- presentation of People's Pro Bono Awards with the MSBA Special Committee on Pro Bono Legal Services at the MSBA Annual Meeting. The awards highlight the extraordinary work of individual volunteers, law firms, members of the judiciary and pro bono legal services programs
- spotlights of award recipients and other volunteers through television news and local press
- creation and celebration of Access to Justice Day honoring Maryland leaders. First honoree - Congressman Benjamin L. Cardin
- special pre-game ceremony at Oriole Park at Camden Yards before a crowd of 40,000 fans

LAWYER SATISFACTION

Attorney satisfaction with their pro bono work has been consistently high. When surveyed, 89% of those working with programs indicated that they would volunteer again. The vast majority felt that their work was both personally rewarding and valuable to their clients. In fact, the most common reasons given for undertaking pro bono work were self-fulfillment and the desire to "give something back to the community."

"I do pro bono work for the same reasons I do commercial litigation. It's just part of who I am, what I've learned, and what I want to do. We sometimes lose connection to personal values. My pro bono cases offer an opportunity for me to have some personal self expression in the work that I do...I also think it helps sustain an interest level in the law. It keeps one alert and learning new things and ultimately I think, that is what makes a lawyer successful."

> "Without a strong organization at the center of this pro bono effort, many of the provider organizations in Maryland would have been misdirected and ineffective in their missions...With PPBAC's commitment in providing the Project with volunteers, our recruiting efforts were greatly decreased, which allowed us to concentrate on...placing cases."
>
> Baltimore Bar Pro Bono Project

> "I honestly do not know what I'd do without PPBAC."
>
> House of Ruth Domestic Violence Legal Clinic

Responding to Changing Community Needs

Under the Maryland Legal Services Corporation guidelines, at least 25% of Maryland's population, an estimated 1 million people in the state, are eligible for free civil legal services. Since the inception of the Action Center, the number of pro bono cases handled has more than tripled. However, it is increasingly evident that the legal services community will need to look towards alternative approaches to serve the larger community.

Community Education and Outreach

The Action Center is engaged in several community education and outreach projects and compiles legal resource directories such as the comprehensive *Guide to Legal Services in Maryland*. Several thousand copies of the *Guide* were distributed to courthouses, libraries, social services agencies and legal services organizations around the state.

With seed money from an ABA mini-grant, the Action Center created a Legal Education and Access for Newcomers (LEAN) program in which volunteer lawyers teach basic familiarity with legal rights and distribute legal resource directories and brochures compiled by the Action Center. The LEAN program was selected as one of three innovative projects nationwide and showcased at the 1995 National Conference of Bar Presidents' Annual Meeting.

Legal services providers, the judiciary and community groups have requested assistance reaching unserved clients. In response, the Action Center has undertaken several new initiatives to help increase access to the law:

- recruitment and coordination of volunteer attorneys to staff citizenship workshops throughout the state and assist lawful permanent residents obtain their citizenship status. Through these workshops, volunteers have assisted over 1500 people become United States citizens
- assistance in the design of the Family Law Pro Se Project with the Administrative Office of the Courts. The Action Center recommended the development of the Women's Law Center's hotline to assist with the domestic relations *pro se* forms
- publication of the first *Maryland Family Law Resource Guide* as well as an abbreviated legal resource list distributed to the public through the clerks' offices of the Circuit Courts
- expansion of an automatic advanced waiver of filing fees for clients of all legal services providers in the state

The People's Pro Bono Action Center is the statewide clearinghouse and coordinator of volunteer legal services. By centralizing the recruitment, recognition, training and promotional activities for private bar involvement, the Action Center is able to enhance the work of the existing legal services programs and prevent duplication of effort.

An evaluation of Maryland's pro bono system by a nationally reknowned legal services consultant concluded that offering expertise, maintaining coordination and facilitating communication among the providers were key roles for the Action Center. The report, *Furthering the Pro Bono Commitment in Maryland: An Assessment of the State's Volunteer Legal Services Delivery System*, concluded that the system's diversity was one of its "fundamental strengths," but stressed continued efforts for coordinated program development.

The Action Center provides information and support for program development through Pro Bono Coordinating Council meetings, educational workshops, and conferences. Approximately once a year, the Action Center organizes a one day Pro Bono Summit bringing together legal services program staff, Board members, and volunteers. Participants explore ways in which they can improve their programs and enhance project collaboration.

Additional support and coordination of activities include:

- development and coordination of a Nuts & Bolts Workshop on Establishing and Operating an Effective Pro Bono Program and the compilation of a "How to" manual
- planning and co-sponsorship of a volunteer management workshop for 20 legal services programs
- organization and coordination of Pro Bono Opportunities Fairs for legal services providers to showcase their programs to young lawyers

In 1993, the Action Center was selected as the local coordinator for the ABA Pro Bono Conference and provided scholarships to nine legal services providers.

BROKERING PARTNERSHIPS BETWEEN PROVIDERS AND BAR GROUPS

The Action Center successfully matches providers with specialty bars or state and local bar sections. Examples include brokering partnerships between the Maryland Disability Law Center and the Maryland Trial Lawyers Association in public accommodation cases; the MSBA Section on Litigation and the House of Ruth for work on domestic violence; and the Young Lawyers Section of both the Bar Association of Baltimore City and MSBA for assistance with the Legal Aid Bureau's *Pro Se* Divorce Clinic.

"The People's Pro Bono Action Center is playing an indispensable role in expanding services by the private bar to Maryland's poor."

Robert J. Rhudy,
Executive Director
Maryland Legal
Services Corporation

"The People's Pro Bono Action Center has been, and continues to be, critical to the success of the pro bono effort in the state. We have come to depend on the Action Center for its leadership and guidance in developing policies and implementing programs for private bar involvement. There is no doubt that the Action Center has helped bring the state closer to ensuring the ideal of equal access to the law."

Robert C. Murphy, Chief Judge Court of Appeals of Maryland

Fulfilling Professional Responsibility

The Maryland Bar considers pro bono legal work the "highest form of professionalism." Rule 6.1 of the Rules of Professional Conduct states that "a lawyer should render public interest legal service." This includes professional services at no fee or reduced fee to persons of limited means, to charitable organizations, to the legal profession, or by financial support to a legal services provider. Since the People's Pro Bono Campaign, pro bono work in Maryland has been equated with free legal service to low-income clients or non-profit organizations serving economically disadvantaged communities.

The Action Center has attempted to instill a sense of professional ethic into those entering the law and ensure that the practicing bar is given ample opportunity to fulfill its professional obligation. The Action Center has presented at the new lawyers' Course on Professionalism and developed a curriculum on pro bono publico taught at the University of Baltimore and the University of Maryland Schools of Law. The Action Center is also relied upon by the organized bar for guidance in policy matters related to pro bono involvement.

The MSBA delegated the responsibility of monitoring and tracking the progress of the voluntary pro bono effort to the Action Center. To date it has reported twice to the Court of Appeals of Maryland. Given the crisis in legal services, assessing the level of pro bono activity and evaluating its impact on the client community may become more critical.

Conclusion

The People's Pro Bono Action Center is at the core of an effective network of legal services providers facing a challenging fiscal environment. Rarely have resources been more restricted and the need for private bar involvement greater. The Action Center is uniquely qualified to bring together diverse strategies and innovative programs to ensure that civil legal services remain a viable mechanism for equal access to the justice system irrespective of socioeconomic constraints. Through a coordinated, cooperative approach with the providers and the bar's fulfillment of it's professional responsibility for pro bono service, the Action Center will strive to accomplish its mission.

TEXAS LAWYERS CARE

PURPOSE

The Texas Lawyers Care Pro Bono/Private Bar Involvement Project was created in 1982. The program assists in the development and expansion of pro bono and private bar projects designed to ensure legal representation for low income clients.

ASSISTANCE PROVIDED

The project can assist in the assessment of local needs and resources. Materials on types of programs statewide and nationwide can be provided as well as sample forms, recruitment brochures, training methods, case referral systems and fund raising possibilities.

Local groups are assisted in designing a program to complement local needs and resources. Speakers for formal presentations to local bar associations, human service agencies, legal services groups, law school classes, and other groups can be arranged. Follow up assistance includes program assessment and evaluation. Grant information and assistance is provided.

Training for volunteer lawyers, pro bono/private bar involvement coordinators and support staff is developed and coordinated by the project. The project can arrange for consultants from the American Bar Association, the State Bar of Texas, law schools, and existing successful programs in Texas and other states.

Books, materials and manuals can be obtained from the project. CLE videotapes for use by programs for training of volunteers and legal services lawyers are available on a loan basis from Texas Lawyers Care through existing pro bono/private bar involvement projects.

Applications for the Emeritus Attorney Program are processed through Texas Lawyers Care. This program allows attorneys who reside in Texas but are not licensed in Texas to do pro bono legal services for low income persons through an approved organization.

ASSISTANCE PROVIDED TO

Local Bar Associations

Local Legal Services Groups

Judiciary

Existing Pro Bono/Private Bar Involvement Projects

Non Attorney Law-Related Professionals

Law Student Groups

Human Service Agencies

FURTHER INFORMATION

(Please call, write or use attached card)

Texas Lawyers Care
State Bar of Texas
P.O. Box 12487
Austin, Texas 78711

(512) 463-1544

PLEASE CHECK THE MATERIALS YOU WISH TO RECEIVE, DETACH AND MAIL OR CALL (512) 463-1544

- ☐ Pro bono opportunities in my community
- ☐ Planning and implementing a pro bono/private bar involvement project
- ☐ Private attorney recruitment
- ☐ Government attorney involvement
- ☐ Corporate attorney involvement
- ☐ Judicial involvement
- ☐ Emeritus attorney program
- ☐ *Neighborhood Clinic Manual*
- ☐ CLE videotapes for volunteer lawyers
- ☐ Training for volunteers
- ☐ Non-attorney recruitment
- ☐ Special projects for
  ☐ the homeless ☐ the elderly ☐ persons with AIDS
- ☐ Other ______

Name ______

Bar/Organization ______

Business Address ______

City ______ State ______ Zip ______

Business Telephone ______

Date ______

THE IDAHO VOLUNTEER LAWYERS PROGRAM

PART I

A. MISSION

The mission of the Idaho Volunteer Lawyers Program (IVLP) is to increase the availability of legal services to the state's poor through the use of volunteer lawyers. The program acts as a legal safety net for the poor by providing free direct legal services.

B. THE NEED

The need to provide increased free legal services to the poor in Idaho is undeniable.

Estimates from the 1990 U.S. Census show that the number of people living below the poverty level in Idaho has risen to 130,588. Over 73,500 of these individuals are children under the age of 16; 13,223 are senior citizens.

If only 25% of the poor in the population group identified as living below the poverty level, or 32,647 individuals, require legal services once during the year (a conservative estimate according to national American Bar Association studies), this figure will far exceed the legal delivery systems' present capacity to serve.

At the present time, there are a total of three programs in Idaho which provide free civil legal services to the poor. One program, the Coalition of Advocates for the Disabled, Inc. (Co-Ad), limits the availability of free legal services to the developmentally disabled who confront legal problems related to their disability. Co-Ad is funded through grants from the state and federal governments as well as private donations.

The main provider of free civil legal services to low-income Idaho residents is the federally-funded Idaho Legal Aid Services, Inc. (ILAS). Priorities for ILAS include representation in housing cases, public entitlement cases, health-care related cases, and, to a limited extent, divorce cases where spousal or child abuse is present.

The IVLP's role in the provision of legal services to Idaho's poor is to complement the services provided by these other programs. The IVLP provides volunteer legal assistance in those type of high priority civil cases for which legal help is not available through either ILAS or Co-Ad. These cases include post divorce actions involving allegations of spousal or child abuse, divorce actions involving allegations of spousal abuse where there are no children present in the home, guardianship/child protection act/termination of parental rights cases, wills/living wills/powers of attorney, and debt collection/bankruptcy/consumer cases.

C. PROGRAM PERFORMANCE

During 1992, the IVLP received over 2,400 requests for case representation from low-income Idahoans. Of this total, 1,157 high priority cases were selected and provided free legal services through the IVLP. This number includes 158 cases in which volunteer attorneys represented Guardians ad Litem in Child Protective Act cases on behalf of over 350 allegedly abused or neglected children. The number of accepted cases also includes 26 cases involving non-profit groups dedicated to helping the poor, elderly, handicapped or otherwise disadvantaged.

In addition to direct case representation for eligible clients, the IVLP also sponsors monthly Advice and Consultation Clinics at the Boise, the Mountain Home, and the Idaho Falls Senior Centers. At the clinics, a volunteer attorney gives legal advice to senior citizens who sign up in advance to talk to the lawyer about their legal problems. Volunteer attorneys served approximately 148 seniors at Advice and Consultation Clinics in 1992.

In cooperation with the Young Lawyers Section of the Idaho State Bar, the IVLP sponsored four (4) community-based Advice and Consultation Clinics in 1992. Two clinics were held in Boise in May. Additional clinics were held in Idaho Falls in November and in Twin Falls in December. A total of 53 individuals were served at these clinics.

Yet another activity IVLP volunteer attorneys participate in is the Ada County Youth Court program. 55 attorneys worked with over 350 students during 1992 to help make Youth Court a success.

Unfortunately, these figures represent only a small dent in the legal service needs of the poor living in Idaho.

Plans for 1993 include continuing with all of the IVLP's existing programs, as well as expanding the Senior Center Advice & Consultation Clinics and the community-based Advice & Consultation Clinics to more locations and greater frequency statewide. The IVLP is also embarking on a three-step "Future Plan" for program services, which has as its goal increasing the number of clients served by the IVLP throughout the state.

D. HISTORY

The IVLP (formerly known as the Pro Bono Program) was organized by the Idaho State Bar in 1982, and concentrated it services in Ada and Canyon Counties. In late 1983, the program expanded statewide to include each of Idaho's seven judicial districts.

The IVLP was organized in large part in response to massive cuts in federal funding to government-sponsored legal service programs serving the poor. The IVLP, exclusively volunteer, refers eligible cases to private attorneys throughout the State who donate their services at no charge. The IVLP fosters a long-standing tradition in the legal profession of providing public service to the poor. It is founded on the ethical principles and obligations of the profession to provide legal services to those in need, regardless of their ability to pay.

In 1988, the IVLP was transferred from the Idaho State Bar to the Idaho Law Foundation, enabling it to obtain a non-profit organizational status. The IVLP's nine (9) member Steering Committee was dissolved, and a fifteen (15) member Policy Council was formed.

E. THE PANEL

Attorneys volunteering to accept case referrals or participate in other IVLP activities are referred to as the IVLP Panel. As of January 1, 1993, there were approximately 2,136 who are licensed as active members of the Idaho State Bar. **Eleven hundred thirty four** (1,134) or 53% of these attorneys are represented on the IVLP Panel.

In November 1991, members of the Idaho State Bar approved a Resolution recognizing the overwhelming need for legal services among Idaho's poor, and calling on each active member of the State Bar to volunteer at least twenty-five hours of legal service each year to IVLP-referred clients. Throughout 1992, the IVLP conducted a major attorney recruitment campaign, seeking the commitment of the Idaho Bar consistent with the Resolution. As a result, 377 attorneys responded with a Pro Bono Pledge of at least 25 hours per year. Attorney recruitment efforts are ongoing.

In addition to the Panel, the IVLP utilizes non-attorney volunteers including legal assistants, recent law school graduates, data entry clerks, legal secretaries, and other clerical support.

Financial Administration

The Idaho State Bar provides all accounting and audit procedures for the IVLP. All revenues received by the IVLP are accounted for in strict conformance with generally accepted accounting principles. An annual audit is conducted by the Boise CPA firm of Reynolds Stanton and Winkler.

G. THE STAFF

The IVLP staff includes the following: (1) the Director; (2) the Intake/Referral Coordinator; (3) the Assistant Intake/Referral Coordinator; and (4) the Office Manager/Secretary.

The Director, a licensed attorney, is responsible for general administration, attorney recruitment, and oversight of all program activities. The Director reports to the Executive Director of the Idaho Law Foundation. The Intake/Referral Coordinator and the Assistant Intake/Referral Coordinator review all incoming requests for legal assistance and place meritorious and high priority requests with volunteer attorneys. The Intake Staff also coordinates the Advice & Consultation Clinics and the Youth Court sessions. The Office Manager maintains all office and client records and provides clerical support.

The State Bar of New Mexico seeks an extraordinary individual to launch and coordinate the Association's new pro bono project.

The project will involve New Mexico's legal community in a significant effort to supplement existing legal services staff programs by providing volunteer representation to low income individuals in civil matters.

The coordinator will be responsible for leading the project, including all tasks involved in its start up. These duties will include:
-developing system of referral of cases of low income clients;

- developing mechanism for training, monitoring and evaluation of the volunteer representation;

-acting as spokesperson for and representative of the project and of the State Bar with respect to pro bono issues;

- producing periodic and annual reports about the project's work;

- acting as liaison with the private bar, legal services/ legal aid programs, law school, and other legal entities;

- coordinating with the recruitment coordinator in recruiting and retaining the maximum number of volunteer attorneys and other legal support volunteers;

- promoting pro bono services through publication of articles for bar and other publications,

- working with CLE Inc., and other legal services training programs to inform private attorneys on substantive poverty law issues and assisting in keeping them current on new developments in the law;

-

The coordinator will work under the supervision of the Executive Director of the State Bar of New Mexico at the State Bar offices.

The project is being funded for one year under a special grant from the State Bar of New Mexico.

--

Desirable qualifications:

- previous experience in legal services/legal aid setting

-excellent written and oral communication skills

sensitivity to the special needs and issues of low-income persons

- ability to work under stress and handle multiple deadlines and projects simultaneously

- program administration and evaluation

- general office procedures such as bookkeeping and record keeping, filing, etc.

This position is part-time, 20 hours per week, and will be available ___________________.

Send resume of experience and cover letter with salary requirements, to Rufina A. Hernández, Executive Director of the State Bar of New Mexico at Post Office Box 25883, Albuquerque, New Mexico 87125

Deadline: January 15, 1996.

Requirements: Excellent telephone skills, efficient self-starter, excellent organizational skills.

Philadelphia Volunteers for the Indigent Program

Program Description

I. Introduction

Even before the funding cutbacks for legal services programs that began in 1980, there were more indigent clients than legal aid programs could handle. The 1980 Census found that more than 350,000 citizens of Philadelphia lived at or below the federal poverty line. Serving them were the 95 staff attorneys at Community Legal Services (CLS), an organization that leaders of the Philadelphia Bar had helped form 14 years earlier. From 1980 to 1986, as the Administration attempted annually to eliminate all aid to the legal services program, the ranks of Philadelphia's poor grew while the number of CLS staff attorneys was cut in half.

In 1981, the Philadelphia Bar Association formed the Philadelphia Lawyers' Volunteer Action Program (PLVAP) as an independent, not-for-profit corporation. Its sole purpose was to help CLS deliver free legal services to the poor, by providing volunteer private attorneys on a pro bono basis to handle cases that CLS attorneys could not take. Over the four years that followed, more than 1,000 attorneys volunteered their time for the PLVAP program, and more than 1,500 clients received free legal assistance through PLVAP.

In 1986, the Board of Governors of the Philadelphia Bar Association and the Board of Trustees of CLS entered into a new partnership to guarantee the expansion of the Bar's pro bono effort. Called Philadelphia VIP, the Program offers all members of the legal community -- partners, associates, paralegals, court reporters, title insurers, experts arbitrators, and mediators among them -- the opportunity to put their talents to much-needed use in virtually every area of law. Philadelphia VIP volunteers serve indigent clients in many contexts: at hearings and trials, in negotiations, at arbitrations, in the library, and on the telephone.

Today, more than 400,000 Philadelphians fall within the class of our poorest citizens, entitling them to free legal services. That entitlement, however, means little if there are not enough lawyers available to provide the services they need. As in past years, Philadelphia VIP -- and its dedicated volunteers -- fill the gap between CLS resources and community need. Your service as a VIP volunteer is vital to that effort.

II. How the Program Works

All cases referred to Philadelphia VIP volunteers are screened twice, first to ensure that the client is income-eligible for the Program, and then to ensure legal merit. Each case is prepared so that the volunteer will know immediately what is involved in handling the referral. The VIP staff contacts as many prospective volunteers as it takes to find a person willing and able to take the case and provide the client with the same high standard of professional service as is offered to fee-paying clients. After the referral is made, the staff checks with each volunteer from time to time, to determine the status of the case and find out whether any support services are needed. When the representation ends, the volunteer is asked to "bill" the Program for the services rendered (that is, report the hours spent on the representation). Throughout the course of the representation, the volunteer is covered by Philadelphia VIP's professional liability insurance, which is primary to the volunteer's own insurance.

What kinds of cases a volunteer can expect to receive depends upon the interests of the volunteer and the needs of VIP's clients. Volunteers are asked to complete a questionnaire to indicate the kinds of cases in which they have a particular interest. Every effort is made to match the volunteer's interests with the client's needs. If a particular referral does not appeal to the volunteer, either because of subject matter or time constraints, the volunteer may simply decline the referral. Every volunteer is asked to accept a least one case each year, but volunteers may be asked to accept additional referrals depending upon the nature of the cases they are handling and the volunteer's willingness and ability to accept additional matters.

III. Support Services

Philadelphia VIP volunteers are not alone. Every volunteer attorney has the opportunity to work with co-counsel, if desired. There is a panel of legal experts available for consultation in virtually every area of the law. Paralegals are also available to assist attorneys on larger matters, and attorneys are available to assist paralegal volunteers who are handling matters in which representation by an advocate other than a licensed attorney is permitted.

Members of the Pennsylvania Shorthand Reporters Association provide VIP volunteers with court reporting and transcription services at reduced or no cost. Volunteer attorneys who need court reporters should call the agency they regularly use, explain that they are representing a client referred through Philadelphia VIP, and request the assignment of a pro bono reporter. If the agency cannot provide a pro bono reporter, the volunteer should call the VIP office, which will arrange for reporting services.

Title insurance companies, real estate appraisers, medical experts, investigators and other subject matter experts, as well as mediators, are also available through the Program on a low- or no-cost basis. VIP volunteers who need services from such experts should call the VIP office to find out what is available for a specific referral. If the volunteer incurs any out-of-pocket costs, VIP may be able to provide some reimbursement (up to a specified maximum). If not, the volunteer will be given a receipt acknowledging the costs as a contribution to the Program, which makes the cost a charitable gift deductible for income tax purposes.

In addition, Philadelphia VIP offers its volunteers excellent training sessions conducted by experts in various fields of the law. A schedule of upcoming sessions is available at the VIP office. Also available is a library of resource books, including sample pleadings, forms, and other literature helpful in the representation of VIP clients.

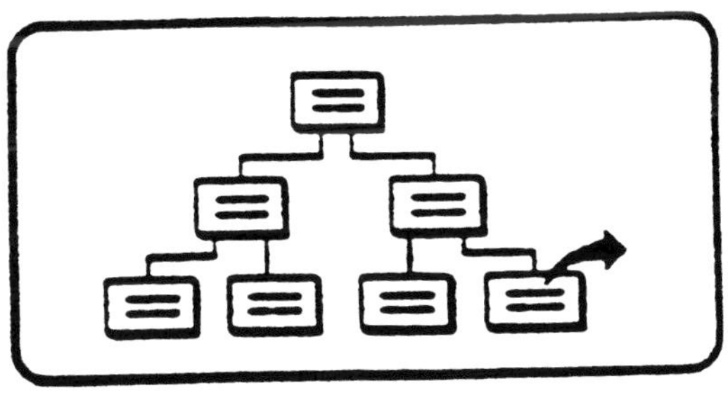

IV. Philadelphia VIP's Staff and Funding

Philadelphia VIP is staffed by two attorneys -- an Executive Director and a Staff Attorney -- and two Program Coordinators, who run the Program on a day-to-day basis and make all referrals. They are supported by one full-time and one part-time secretary.

The staff is supervised by a Board of Directors comprised of client representatives, members of the public interest bar, trustees of Community Legal Services, Bar Association officers, judges, law professors, and attorneys from law firms large and small. The Chancellor of the Philadelphia Bar Association and the Executive Directors of both the Bar Association and CLS also serve ex officio on the Board. All appointments to the Board are made by the Chancellor, and are confirmed by the Bar's Board of Governors.

Philadelphia VIP is an independent entity, qualified as a charitable corporation under Section 501(c) of the Internal Revenue Code. It was created through grants from the Philadelphia Bar Foundation, Community Legal Services, and the Philadelphia Bar

Association. VIP is funded on an ongoing basis by grants from these groups, as well as other sources, including: Donor Option contributions through United Way (VIP does not receive United Way grants from undesignated contributions); direct contributions; and grants from public authorities and private foundations. The Program also receives limited finding from attorney fee awards in VIP cases. Such awards, net of any unreimbursed costs incurred by the volunteer attorney or firm, generally belong to VIP, though adjustments to this rule may be made in appropriate cases.

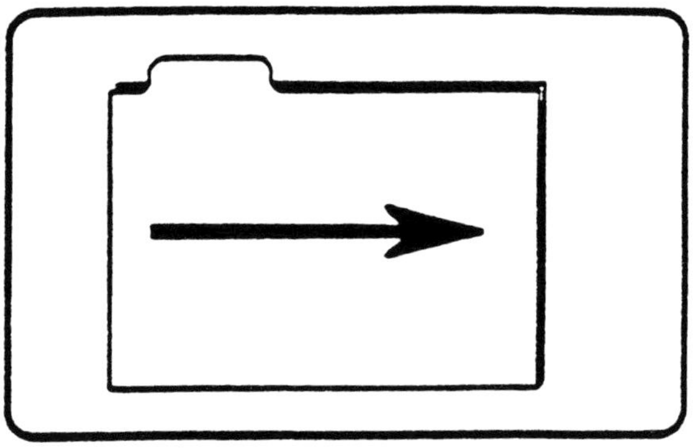

V. The Referral Process

The referral process, illustrated graphically on the chart on page 8, generally works like this:

1. Most clients referred to VIP are identified through the regular intake process at Community Legal Services (CLS). Clients are screened for financial eligibility, case type and potential legal merits. (Attached as Appendix A are the current income eligibility guidelines used in this screening process.)

2. CLS then refers the case to VIP. After additional screening for legal merit, referral to a volunteer will be made. The volunteer is contacted by telephone -- directly, or through VIP's designated "contact persons" in certain larger firms -- and is asked to accept the case. Every effort is made to match the volunteer with a particular type of case that he or she requested.

3. Both the client and the volunteer are sent letters confirming the referral. Generally, the client's letter (Appendix B) tells the client that if he or she fails to contact the volunteer attorney within 14 days, he or she may be disqualified from the Program. (In some exceptional situations, the volunteer is asked to contact the client, but this would be specified in the referral letter.) If the client does not contact the volunteer within 14 days, VIP asks the volunteer to send a letter (Appendix C) to the client, reminding the client that he or she must contact the lawyer right away, so that the lawyer can represent the client effectively. The volunteer's letter and Case Referral Sheet (Appendices D and E) contain information about the client and the facts of the case. The referral sheet also includes the name of an attorney or paralegal from CLS who can be contacted for advice or back-up assistance. (CLS provides such assistance unless it represents the adverse party in the matter and is precluded by the conflict from doing so.) Also included in the referral packet is a Closing Form (Appendix F), which must be completed by the volunteer and returned to VIP after six months or when the case is closed. (Sorry, but we cannot avoid this "red tape" requirement. The Legal Services Corporation, which is the major

government funding source for CLS, requires client and service information on all cases closed by private attorneys doing volunteer work for clients referred by CLS.)

4. VIP also asks the volunteer attorney to fill out a very short questionnaire two months after the referral is made (Appendix G).

5. If the volunteer attorney is unable to handle the case for any reason, such as a client conflict, he or she should contact one of the Program Coordinators by telephone immediately:

   a. If the volunteer decides not to handle a case when it is first referred, the volunteer should complete the Closing Form, indicating as the reason for case closure, "Volunteer Will Not Handle." This completed sheet, along with the entire referral packet, should be returned to the VIP office immediately.

   b. If the volunteer is willing to handle the case, pending the initial client interview and his/her review of the case, but contact between volunteer and client is not made within 14 days or in response to the volunteer's follow-up letter, the volunteer should complete the Closing Form, indicating as the reason for case closure, "Client Did Not Make Contact." The Closing Form should be returned to VIP.

   c. If after interviewing the client and the case the volunteer has any doubts about the client's eligibility, the merits of the case, or a similar concern, the volunteer should contact one of the Program Coordinators. If the volunteer decides not to handle the case, the Closing Form should be completed, indicating the appropriate reason for case closure, and returned to VIP.

6. The client and attorney are encouraged to enter into a written agreement concerning the representation. This will make their respective responsibilities clear, and fulfill any obligations that may exist under Rule of Professional Conduct 1.5. A standard form for such an agreement is attached as Appendix H.

7. Court costs for most VIP clients can be waived or avoided by proceeding in forma pauperis ("IFP"). Standard forms to proceed IFP are attached for federal court (Appendix I), for most state court civil cases (Appendix J), and for divorce cases, where leave of court must be obtained by petition and rule (Appendix K). If waiver is not possible, VIP has limited funding available for some costs. More importantly, as noted above, VIP has recruited court reporters, title companies and other agencies to provide litigation support, on a low- or no-cost basis, for VIP cases. Requests by a volunteer attorney for reimbursement of costs and expenses should be made to the Executive Director, after the attorney determines that the costs cannot be waived or paid by the client, but before the costs are incurred.

8. After the case has been accepted, handled, and closed, the volunteer completes the Closing Form and returns it to VIP. (A volunteer may decide to terminate representation in a particular matter after a discrete phase of the representation has been completed, e.g., after discovery, negotiation or arbitration but before trial, after trial but before appeal, etc. However, this must be made clear to the client at the outset of the representation, so that

the client can protect his or her interests.)

9. Clients are asked to evaluate VIP, too. (See Appendix L). With your comments, ar the clients' responses, we hope to make our program as responsive and efficie as possible.

In summary, these are the responsibilities of CLS, VIP, and the volunteer attorney in the referral process:

1. CLS Responsibilities

a. Determine financial eligibility.
b. Determine if the client's problem can/should be handled by VIP.
c. Screen the case for potential legal merit.
d. Refer the case to VIP.
e. Provide back-up assistance and advice.

2. VIP Responsibilities

a. Screen the case for potential legal merit.
b. Refer the case to a volunteer lawyer.
c. Inform the client and referring attorney of the referral.
d. Provide back-up assistance and advice.
e. Track cases and their outcomes.
f. Arrange for free or low-cost support services.
g. Approve requests for reimbursement of costs, or acknowledge as charitable contributions any unreimbursed costs.
h. Coordinate training programs and materials.
i. Recruit volunteers.
j. Handle complaints from attorneys or clients.

3. Volunteer's Responsibilities

a. Accept the case referred by VIP Coordinators.
b. Handle the case in a timely, professional manner.
c. Complete and return the Referral Form within 30 days after receiving the referral.
d. Consult with the CLS resource attorney or paralegal, if needed.
e. Keep the VIP staff advised of any problems that are encountered.
f. Complete and return the Status/Closing Form six months after receiving the referral, or when the case is closed.

The VIP Referral Process

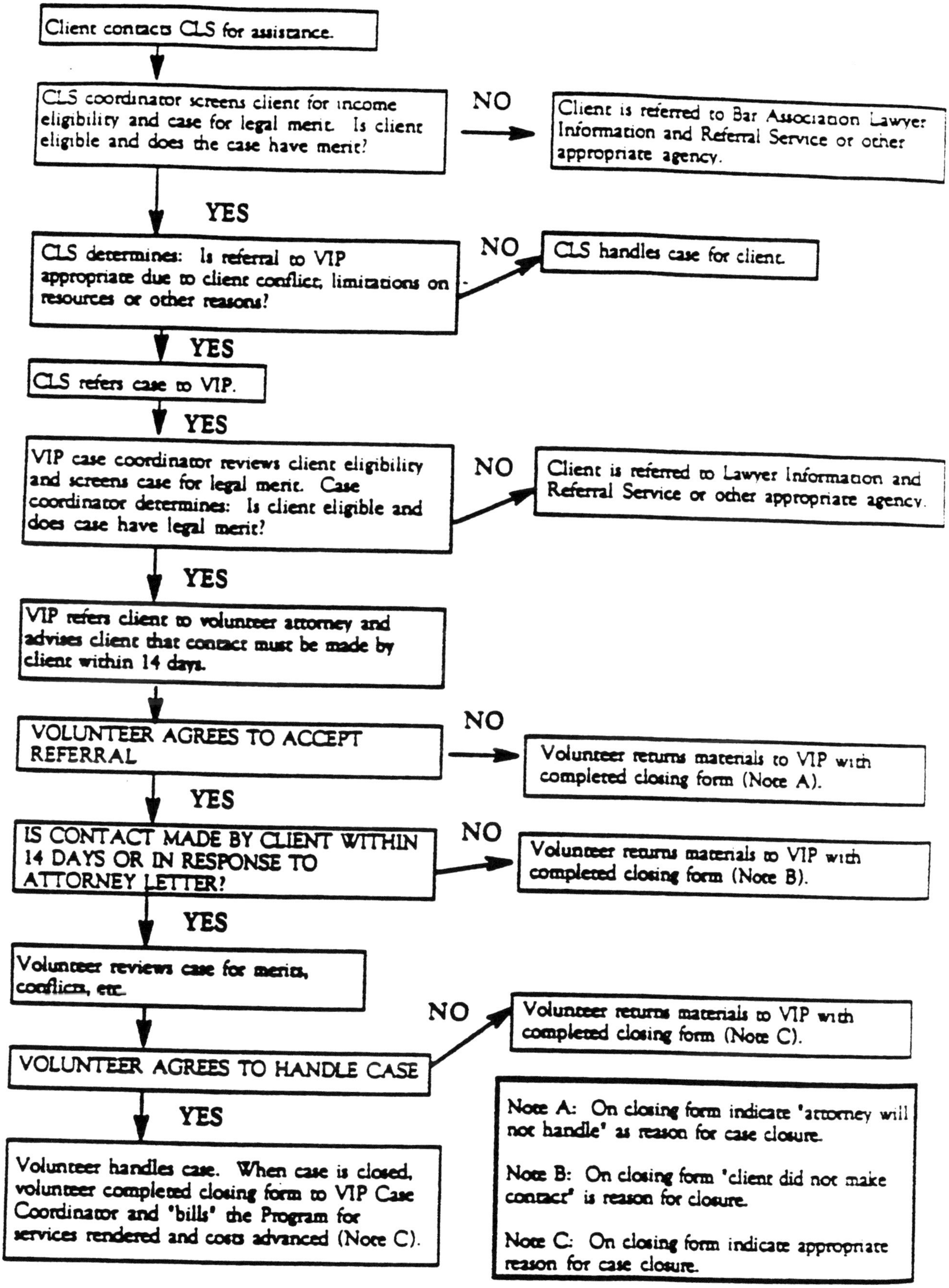

LEGAL AID SOCIETY OF THE ORANGE COUNTY BAR ASSOCIATION, INC.
PRO BONO PROGRAM 1996

CASEWORK

CONSUMER: All consumer related issues are referred through the pro bono panel. Bankruptcy, Chapter 7 and 13, are the areas of most frequent referral and one where new attorneys are needed. Car repossession and deficiency judgment cases, used car sales and repair disputes, debt and contract disputes, are some of the types of cases referred. About 200 consumer cases were referred in 1995. For more information, please contact Cathy Tucker, Pro Bono Coordinator

FAMILY: This is the area of the greatest number of requests for services, primarily dissolution of marriage with custody and child support issues. There are also paternity/custody disputes, enforcement of support and post judgment custody disputes. There is an increasing number of guardianship cases for minor children and for adults. There were almost 600 family cases referred in 1995. About 250 attorneys will handle divorces. Many of them accept three cases. New attorneys are always needed. Training will be offered in the Spring of 1996, and manuals are provided. For more information, please contact Cathy Tucker, Pro Bono Coordinator.

GUARDIAN AD LITEM PROGRAM: Pro bono attorneys and lay volunteers serve as advocates for children in the juvenile, criminal and domestic relations division of the circuit court. The majority of cases involve abused, abandoned, and neglected children who are the subject of juvenile dependency cases. GALs are appointed in domestic relations cases involving divorce, paternity, and post judgment disputes. The role of the GAL and the GAL Volunteer Assistant is to serve as the "eyes and ears" of the Court and to advocate for the best interests of the child. Currently over 3500 children in Orange County are represented through the GAL Program. Approximately 300 attorneys and 80 lay volunteers participate. Training will be offered in the Spring of 1996, manuals are available. For more information please contact Susan Khoury, Program Coordinator.

HOUSING: A variety of housing and housing related cases are referred. Eviction defense of a private landlord/tenant rental is the most common referral. There are also disputes over conditions of the rental unit, occasionally eviction defense of federally subsidized housing, mortgage foreclosures, boundary disputes, fraudulent transfers, all related to the homestead of the client. About 150 housing cases were referred in 1995. For more information, please contact Cathy Tucker, Pro Bono Coordinator.

****

PROJECTS

AIDS PROJECT: A special will panel provides simple wills and related documents to persons with AIDS, ARC, and who are HIV positive. Attorneys interview clients at support groups such as AIDS Resource Alliance and Hope and Help. Participation requires four sessions of interviews. A training will be offered in January or February of 1996. 22 slots. For more information, please contact Cathy Tucker, Pro Bono Coordinator.

ATTORNEYS FIGHTING FOR SERIOUSLY ILL CHILDREN: Attorneys will provide assistance for families with children who are suffering from a critical illness. These families in crisis need help with insurance, wills, trusts, credit and bankruptcy information, review of real estate documents and other issues. Panel attorneys will not do litigation, but provide advice, counseling, negotiation, etc. A mentor panel will be available for expert assistance. Bryant Applegate, an attorney with Orange County, serves as volunteer liaison. Preference will be given to government attorneys and corporate counsel; 15 slots. For more information, please contact Cathy Tucker, Pro Bono Coordinator.

CITIZEN DISPUTE SETTLEMENT/FAMILY MEDIATION: Attorneys serve as mediators for the OCBA sponsored programs of CDS and Family Mediation. For CDS, attorneys agree to act as mediators for disputes over civil matters such as neighborhood disputes, landlord/tenant, etc. For Family Mediation, attorneys with specific training requirements act as mediators in family law matters. Preference for participation for pro bono credit is given to government attorneys and corporate counsel. There is a limited number of slots for private attorneys. Because a schedule is needed by mid-January, slots are assigned on a first come, first serve basis: 45 slots for CDS, 22 slots for Family Mediation. Attorneys should expect to be available for 10 sessions. For more information, please contact Cathy Tucker, Pro Bono Coordinator.

COMMUNITY EDUCATION PANEL: Government attorneys (assistant state attorneys, public defenders, city and county attorneys) and in-house corporate counsel agree to speak to community groups and participate in community programs such as festivals and fairs that impact low income residents of Orange County. Attorneys speak on a variety of topics and discuss the Legal Aid Society as well. For more information, please contact Alana Brenner, Community Education Project Coordinator.

EARNED INCOME CREDIT/TAX ASSISTANCE PROJECT: Attorneys will provide assistance to eligible clients in preparing their returns, especially to obtain the earned income tax credit. Training will be provided. There will be several nights during the January-April period during which this assistance will be provided. Preference will be given to government attorneys and corporate counsel: 10 slots. For more information, please contact Alana Brenner, Community Education Project Coordinator.

HOMELESS ADVOCACY PROJECT: This project began its pro bono component in 1992. Attorneys conduct intake at a variety of food and shelter sites around the Orange County area each month. Cases identified for specific legal assistance can be handled by the interviewing attorney or referred through the pro bono panel; 45 participants are needed. There will be a training in January 1996. For more information, please contact Helaine Blum, Homeless Advocacy Project Coordinator.

TEEN COURT: This diversion program was created to help juveniles who have been accused of misdemeanors. The juveniles will appear at a teen court composed of other teens as prosecutor, defense attorney, and jury. Pro bono attorneys will serve as advisors and trainers. There are 35 slots available on a first come basis for attorneys. Preference will be given to judges, government and corporate attorneys. Attorneys should expect to be available for 12 sessions or about 30 hours. For more information, please contact Cathy Tucker, Pro Bono Coordinator.

C:\PROBONO\PROGRAM

Put Something Back

A Joint Pro Bono Project of the Eleventh Judicial Circuit and the Dade County Bar Association

June 13, 1996

"Put Something Back" is the official pro bono project for Dade County. Since 1981, Put Something Back has conducted pro se divorce clinics designed to assist low income persons on how to represent themselves in court.

"Pro Se Divorce Clinics" are held once per month at the Dade County Courthouse during lunchtime. Clients are pre-screened by a staff attorney and once it is determined that they qualify, they are invited to the next clinic. At each clinic, the litigants first view a video on dissolution of marriage in Florida. Next, they complete forms necessary to file for divorce with the assistance of pro bono attorneys. Before they leave, they are given the name and telephone number of a staff attorney who is "on duty" to handle that month's questions.

123 Northwest First Avenue . Miami, Florida 33128 . (305) 579-5733 . FAX (305) 372-7693

**Volunteer Legal Services Project
of Monroe County, Inc.
Rochester, NY**

Description of Debt Collection Advice Clinic

VLSP's debt collection advice clinic is held bi-weekly from 5 PM to 7 PM at the VLSP office. The after hours clinic is convenient for clients who work during the day. Sixteen clients are scheduled at fifteen minute intervals. We open scheduling for each clinic one week before the clinic. Three volunteer attorneys are scheduled to meet with clients at the clinic. Clients are instructed to bring a list of debts to the clinic.

When a client arrives, s/he is handed a document which describes what will happen at the clinic. The client is asked to complete a screening questionnaire which, when completed, enables the volunteer attorney to see the client's financial situation at a glance. After the form is completed, the client meets privately with one of the clinic volunteers for 15-20 minutes.

Approximately 80% of clients coming to the clinic have no income or assets which can be executed against to collect judgments. Yet the clients are invariably scared and confused about summons, subpoenas, their credit, etc. The volunteers advise these clients what creditors can and cannot do to collect judgments. Credit implications are discussed. We have developed a handout which reinforces the information given at the session. We also give clients the brochure on collection published by the National Consumer Law Center.

VLSP has developed a "cease and desist" letter which clients can use to invoke the protection of the Fair Debt Collection Practices Act. Clients are given this letter with instructions on how and in what circumstances to use it.

Those clients with significant debt who have income or assets subject to execution are given a bankruptcy screening questionnaire which they are asked to complete at home and return to VLSP. When the form is returned, it is reviewed by a VLSP staff attorney to ensure that the case fits VLSP's criteria for bankruptcy representation. If so, a file is opened and the case referred to a volunteer attorney.

We ask all debt clinic volunteers to complete a report on each client they see. We ask the volunteer to outline advice given to each client. We also invite volunteers to identify legal representation needed by the client other than bankruptcy and questions that the client had that the volunteer was unable to handle. VLSP staff follow up if more representation is needed or questions need to be answered.

ABA CENTER FOR PRO BONO
Exchange

PRIVATE BAR INVOLVEMENT IN LEGAL SERVICES FOR THE POOR   VOLUME 14, NUMBER 3 • JUNE 1996

Court–Based Pro Bono

by Robert M. Elardo and Carl R. Poirot

Illustration by Jim Starr

Collaboration between pro bono programs and the court system, including locating all or part of a pro bono program within the courthouse, is becoming increasingly more common. As resources shift, pro bono program/court partnerships can be an effective strategy for maximizing resources. These partnerships can provide unique intake, placement, recruitment, volunteer networking and publicity opportunities. The following are descriptions of the court–based pro bono projects of the Erie County Bar Association Volunteer Lawyers Project and the San Diego Volunteer Lawyer Program.

Erie County Bar Association Volunteer Lawyers Project

Erie County Bar Association Volunteer Lawyers Project (VLP) is located in Buffalo, New York and serves clients throughout Erie County. VLP has 850 attorneys who are active participants in the program. Most of those attorneys receive their pro bono referrals from VLP in the traditional referral method and work on the cases out of their own office. However, an increasing number of attorneys now are working with VLP's special projects.

The common threads that weave VLP's special projects together are that they attempt to involve more attorneys, serve more clients and require less pro bono program staff time and involvement than the traditional method of a pro bono program calling an individual attorney to take an individual case. VLP's court–based projects have been particularly effective.

(continued on next page)

Attorney of the Morning—Landlord/Tenant

VLP's Attorney of the Morning Program (AOM) provides representation to low income tenants who are faced with evictions in Buffalo City Court. The program operates on Mondays, Wednesdays and Fridays. On each of those days, an attorney who has been trained in landlord/tenant law is scheduled to be the AOM.

In this program, VLP meets the clients for the first time right at the court house. The goal is to help prevent their becoming homeless. Prior to the initiation of this program, the court estimated that 90 percent of unrepresented tenants were evicted without even being granted additional time with which to move out and avoid becoming homeless.

VLP keeps track of the results that it actually achieves for clients. These "result codes" show how successful AOM has been. Of the cases that VLP represents to conclusion,[1] 19 percent result in the petition being dismissed[2] and 26 percent result in stipulated agreements that save the tenancy and allow the tenant to remain indefinitely. These two very positive results for VLP's clients combine to account for 45 percent of AOM's results.

> *"The extra time that VLP leverages for clients often can be what keeps the client's family from becoming homeless by giving them time to find a new home or to move into a place that they may already have found, but which is not yet available."*

In another 48 percent of the cases, the AOM achieves some benefit or benefits for the tenant, so that in only 7 percent of AOM's cases does the client end up getting evicted with an immediate warrant of eviction and a money judgment. This is particularly impressive when you consider the fact that VLP represents every eligible client, even if they have no substantive or procedural defenses.

The 48 percent of the cases that result in some benefit or benefits for the tenant break down as follows:

- ❑ 18 percent result in extra time to move and a complete avoidance of a money judgment
- ❑ 5 percent result in extra time to move and a reduced money judgment
- ❑ 11 percent result only in extra time to move
- ❑ 13 percent result in no extra time but a complete avoidance of a money judgment
- ❑ 1 percent result in no extra time but reduce the money judgment.

The extra time that VLP leverages for clients often can be what keeps the client's family from becoming homeless by giving them time to find a new home or to move into a place that they may already have found, but which is not yet available. In other cases, the clients are ready to move out and interested only in avoiding a money judgment, if possible.

Ninety–nine attorneys currently are on VLP's landlord/tenant project list, all of whom may be called to act as AOM. In addition, in order to get on the list, lawyers must either attend a live VLP AOM training or view a training

(continued on page

COURT–BASED PRO BONO

(continued from page 2)

video tape and review the handout materials from the training. The tapes and materials are available for attorneys who want a refresher course as well. VLP removes attorneys from its list if it feels that they are inappropriate for continued service as an AOM.

Volunteer law students (sometimes the students receive law school credit for working with VLP) and law graduates act as program coordinators. They are responsible for scheduling the attorneys, reminding the attorneys of their scheduled date, making announcements in the courtroom regarding the program, performing client intake at the courthouse, working with the attorneys on the quick preparation and representation of cases, making appropriate follow up referrals for clients, taking care of follow up paper work and record keeping at VLP's office and reporting to VLP's Managing Attorney on the cases handled and on the operation of the program.

AOM Coordinators must go through the same training as attorneys. In addition, they become familiar with the AOM's Coordinator's Manual, which details their job and procedural responsibilities. When they return from court, VLP's Managing Attorney reviews their files and discusses any difficult or "problem" files with them.

About a week before the attorney is scheduled to be the AOM, the Coordinators mail a reminder letter along with some brief substantive materials. The substantive materials have changed over the years. For the first few years, they consisted of a memo. Approximately one year ago, VLP started using a chart of defenses that one of VLP's volunteers developed and a legal services housing attorney expanded.

At court, VLP usually has two Coordinators. They are armed with the relevant statutes, a landlord/tenant guide and the defenses chart.

The attorneys have found this program very attractive. They are able to schedule their pro bono work ahead of time and block out a few hours in which to do it. There is no follow–up work required of attorneys. As a result, when they leave the court room at lunch time, their work on these cases is completed.

On their scheduled morning, the attorney shows up and begins working with the AOM Coordinators to hear about the cases, find out what result each client desires (i.e., to stay in the apartment or to get some amount of time to move out), and then the attorney begins to negotiate with the landlord or the landlord's attorney. A very high percentage of VLP's cases settle in pre–trial negotiations. In those cases that are not settled, the attorney appears in court that morning with the tenant, raises any defenses and otherwise pleads the tenant's case.

"The extra time that VLP leverages for clients often can be what keeps the client's family from becoming homeless by giving them time to find a new home..."

Cases that are of a more complex variety (e.g., those involving warranty of habitability trials and those involving public and subsidized housing issues) are adjourned and referred to Neighborhood Legal Services (NLS). NLS is the local legal service program and their cooperation in making this program work has been essential. Not only do they pick up most of the more complex cases, but they also have played a large role in the training of the volunteer attorneys. NLS operates a similar program with its staff attorneys on Tuesdays and Thursdays. This ensures that the court is covered each day of the week.

The cooperation of the court also has been a key element in the success of this program. Not only does the court grant adjournments when necessary, but it also has provided VLP with a room in the courthouse on the same floor that these cases are heard. The court allows the AOM Coordinators to make announcements in the courtroom about the fact that the project is there to help low income tenants. The court even refers people for assistance.

Attorney of the Morning Programs are used in landlord/tenant court in approximately eight jurisdictions throughout New York State. In 1990, VLP received a special grant from the New York Interest on Lawyer Account Fund (IOLA) for the operation of this program.

Attorney of the Afternoon—Immigration/Deportation Cases

The Attorney of the Afternoon Program (AOA) operates in much the same way as the AOM program does. AOA provides representation to low income aliens who are in the custody of the Immigration and Naturalization Service (INS) and who are facing deportation or exclusion proceedings in Immigration Court.

Since immigration is such a complex area, VLP has thus far limited participation in this program to attorneys who have prior experience in immigration law. In addition, VLP has provided training in specific issues that attorneys will face in these particular cases.

In a very high percentage of the cases that AOA handles, there is no relief from deportation available for the client. However, even in these cases,

Illustration by Jim Starr

VLP performs valuable services for the clients. The presence of an attorney to explain to the client the lack of options that they have and to help streamline the case can often shorten dramatically the amount of time that the client will remain in custody before being returned to their country.

In addition, there are many cases where a lawyer can make a real difference in a person's life. The volunteer lawyers are able to identify and present defenses, conduct bond hearings to get the clients released from custody, make motions for change of venue to get the cases transferred to where the client's friends and family reside and get adjournments so that more detailed and extensive work can be done on the files.

More cases carry–over from one day to another in this program than in the landlord/tenant area. This leads to more work during the in–between days for the law student coordinator. They are often responsible for conducting factual and legal research and for informing the next Attorney of the Afternoon about what has transpired in a given case.

The cooperation of the INS has been very important for the success of this program. It provides the program with the docket sheet and charging documents ahead of time, brings the clients in earlier in the day so that VLP can interview them and provides VLP with a room out of which to work and in which to interview clients.

The San Diego Volunteer Lawyer Program

The San Diego Volunteer Lawyer Program (SDVLP) is a free–standing pro bono law firm serving indigent residents of San Diego County. SDVLP is co–sponsored by three local bar associations and the Legal Aid Society of San Diego.

SDVLP employs 16 paid staff, including 7 attorneys. In addition to the 3,000 registered volunteers, three volunteer attorneys function as regular, part–time staff attorneys, each with lead responsibility for discrete service components. During 1995, SDVLP provided legal assistance to 20,000 clients.

SDVLP offers legal services in a wide range of civil matters and through

San Diego Volunteer Lawyer Program Staff, Claudia Camacho, assists a client at the Family Law Access Project located at the central San Diego Superior Court.

"The probate court asked SDVLP to establish an in-court clinic to provide pro se guardianship applicants with legal assistance and, in appropriate cases, actual representation in court."

a variety of service delivery methods. In the last several years, more emphasis has been placed on developing out–stationed clinics, preferably right within or in close proximity to a courthouse appropriate to the legal matter at issue.

Domestic Violence Prevention Program

Victims of domestic violence who are unrepresented by counsel receive legal advice, assistance in completing and filing temporary restraining orders and referrals for ongoing representation and related social services at three court sites. Clinics operate daily, five days a week in the main courthouse, four days a week and three days a week respectively at the other two court sites. The program serves a total of approximately 4,500 clients at these sites each year. Volunteers include attorneys, law students and paralegals, all of whom must complete SDVLP's training.

Family Law Access Project

In San Diego County, more than 65 percent of all family matters involve at least one unrepresented party. The vast majority of these persons are indigent or near indigent and, out of economic necessity and the lack of adequate legal services resources, must represent themselves. The Family Law Access Project (FLAP) was created to assist these litigants and to reduce the congestion and inefficiency of the courts resulting from unassisted self–representation.

FLAP assists individuals proceeding *in propria persona* (in pro per or pro se) with legal advice and assistance at whatever stage the litigants might be. The legal assistance provided is thus "unbundled" and the client continues in pro per, unless it is clear that the person is unable, for whatever reason, to proceed alone. The latter clients are referred to SDVLP's ongoing representation panel or, if ineligible, to a bar–sponsored lawyer referral service or modest means panel. In addition, mediation services to both parties are offered and, in fact, are strongly encouraged.

FLAP services are available daily in the two larger family law courthouses, with plans to expand to two additional sites in the coming year. In addition to donated office and counter space at the courts, staffing is funded by the county at the behest of the superior court. In 1995, FLAP assisted more than 12,000 people. This project has received recognition awards from the National Association of Counties and the California Judicial Council. More than 200 volunteer attorneys participate in the project most of whom are from the family law bar. SDVLP provides basic family law and mediation training.

Guardianship Project

In California, the Probate Department of the Superior Court, along with the Probate Examiner's Office, handles applications for guardianship of the pe son and of property. This court had been inundated with pro se applicants for guardianship of the person, usually involving grandchildren or other close relatives. Most of these applicants are indigent and totally unfamiliar with the legal complexities of the guardianship laws and procedures.

The probate court requested SDVLP to establish an in–court clinic to provide these applicants with legal assistance and, in appropriate cases, actual representation in court. The court provided space for the clinic, although the space proved to be inadequate after about six months of operation. As a result, the actual clinic was moved to SDVLP offices less than two blocks from the courthouse.

Clinics are held on Tuesdays and Thursdays, starting at 3:00 p.m. Clients are referred directly from the court or the probate examiner's office. Applicants who are eligible for services are assisted on a first–come basis and those over income are given an information packet and referred to the bar's lawyer referral service. In 1995, 560 applicants were provided with services. The volunteer pool for this project has over 100 attorneys, all of whom have been trained by SDVLP.

Federal Civil Rights Project

The Federal Civil Rights Project was developed at the request of the U.S. District Court, which was interested in offering a legal representation resource to pro per litigants who had already filed a civil rights claim in federal court. The court agreed to refer only those claimants who were indigent, who had filed in the proper court and who had a colorable claim. This project is now in the process of restructuring, since many of the referred claimants were prisoners and evaluating the merits of the claims required too much staff time.

Although SDVLP is still accepting non–prisoner cases, it is hoping to involve a local law school clinic to provide the initial investigation and evaluation. The court provides a small grant to SDVLP to defer out–of–pocket expenses. The volunteer panel consists of the larger law firms who litigate in federal court. The presiding judge was very involved in the design of the project and in the recruitment of volunteer attorneys and law firms.

The court–based programs highlighted in this article are examples of what can happen when pro bono programs and courts work together. The key to the success of these programs is the juxtaposition of pro bono program resources being brought to bear to help meet client and court needs.

Robert M. Elardo is Managing Attorney, Erie County Bar Association.

Carl R. Poirot is Executive Director, San Diego Volunteer Lawyer Program.

Footnotes

[1] The cases in which VLP does not represent the client to conclusion are those in which the client is not eligible, the client withdraws or disappears, the client becomes unduly uncooperative or abusive, or the case is referred. Referrals usually are to Neighborhood Legal Services (NLS) and usually involve public housing, subsidized housing or warranty of habitability hearings. Eight percent of all AOM cases end up being scheduled for a warranty of habitability hearing. Almost all of these cases are referred to NLS.

[2] Statistics are based on combined 1993, 1994 and 1995 cases.

Description of the Women and Children's Poverty Prevention Project

Legal services, alone, rarely provide a client with enough help to change his or her life. VLSP is experimenting with methods of service delivery designed to address the broader issues of a clients' circumstance. The Women and Children's Poverty Prevention Project (WCPPP) promotes a holistic, multi-disciplinary approach to the problems of low-income women and their children. Through service clinics, materials and education, the Project attempts to address the root causes of poverty among women, providing them with access to a wide range of legal, health, vocational/educational and parenting services. The Project is sponsored by the Bar Association of San Francisco Volunteer Legal Services Program (VLSP).

The major accomplishment of the project to date is the **"One Stop" Women's Clinic.** This Clinic offers low income women simultaneous access to a wide range of social, legal, medical, vocational and parenting services in one location, on one date. Between 70 and 140 women attend each clinic (which includes on-site child care); 17 different service providers offer counseling, information, health examinations, resume preparation and workshops throughout the day-long event. Those needing legal representation are referred to VLSP panel attorneys; the other providers present conducted client follow up as desired and arranged by the client.

Women also have a chance to "shop" in a clothes closet full of quality donated clothing, and leave the clinic with a gift bag of donated personal items. (Children at the Clinic with their mothers each go home with a pile of donated books.) On-site child care, lunch, and a prize raffle are other components of the Clinic that make the day both a productive and enjoyable one for the women.

In an effort to make the services offered at the "One Stop" Clinic more fully accessible to non-English speaking women, we offered a bilingual Spanish/English Clinic in December '95. One third of the workshops were presented in Spanish, fifty percent of our service providers were bilingual, and Spanish interpreters were assigned to non Spanish speaking service providers. Also, Spanish interpreters were matched with monolingual Spanish speaking women who attended the Clinic. The Interpreters accompanied their client-partner throughout the day-long program, allowing them to consult with any and all service providers as well as to attend workshops in English. (Spanish-speaking child care workers were also recruited and available at the Clinic.)

We have not only successfully worked to address the needs of low-income women who are culturally diverse, but also diverse in age. Our next Clinic will offer a special focus on the health, vocational, and legal concerns of women over forty and seniors.

We are also developing a mentoring network of professional women who will work with interested women for three months after the Clinic to provide additional guidance and support in implementing the plans they develop during the Clinic.

Client follow-up has revealed that many client's lives have, in fact, been changed as a result of the service-rich Women's Clinic approach. Many have obtained jobs or enrolled in job training. In fact, a job developer who will be presenting a workshop on resume preparation for the May '96 Clinic is a woman who had attended a Clinic two years ago while she was unemployed and living in the projects. She utilized the resume writing services we offered at the Clinic in '94. She credits the Clinic for helping her to get her feet on the ground and making her job search a successful one.

Because client and service provider reaction to the Clinic has been overwhelmingly positive, the Clinic will be held four times a year. This systematic approach to service delivery can be replicated in both rural and urban areas. VLSP would be pleased to assist in replication efforts.

For more information, please contact Tanya Neiman, Director, BASF Volunteer Legal Services Program, 685 Market Street, Suite 700, San Francisco, CA 94105, Tel. (415)764-1600.

Talks & Workshops
(in the Conference Rooms)

Follow the Signs to the Conference Rooms

Morning Session 1

10:30–11:30 a.m.

Title	Presenter	Conf. Room
How to Write a Resume	Marco Gonzalez, Jewish Vocational Services	Library
Domestic Violence: What to Do, Where to Get Help	SFNLAF; The Riley Center	Classroom 1

Morning Session 2

11:45 a.m.–12:45 p.m.

Title	Presenter	Conf. Room
Safe Sex Party	Terry Wheeler, Real Education Demolishing AIDS	Library
Bills, Debts, and Consumer Rip-Offs	Candy Acevedo, Consumer Credit Counselors	Classroom 1

Afternoon Session 3

1:30–2:30 p.m.

Title	Presenter	Conf. Room
What to Do When Your Kids Are Driving You Crazy	T.A.L.K. Line	Library
Are You Ready to Start Your Own Business?	W.I.S.E.	Classroom 1

Schedule

Check-In
Coffee & Pastries
9:15-10:00 a.m.

■

Orientation
10:00-10:15 a.m.

■

Free Services
In the Auditorium
10:15-12:45 p.m.

■

Talks/Workshops
Session 1
10:30-11:30 a.m.

■

Talks/Workshops
Session 2
11:45-12:45 p.m.

■

LUNCH
(Free box lunch available in Auditorium)
12:45-1:30 p.m.

■

More Free Services in the Auditorium
1:30-2:30 p.m.

■

Talks/Workshops
Session 3
1:30-2:30 p.m.

■

Closing Assembly
Raffle
2:30-3:00 p.m.

Free Services
(available all day in the Auditorium)

LEGAL/HOUSING

Legal Advice & Referral: BASF Volunteer Legal Services Program—Attorneys will give legal advice on family issues, landlord/tenant, immigration and other legal matters.

SSI: Screening for SSI (disability) eligibility for kids & adults.

Housing Info: Innovative Housing—Information on shared and transitional housing programs.

HEALTH

Dental Screening: CARECEN—free dental screening.

Birth Control & AIDS Info: Lyon–Martin Women's Health Services—Info on birth control, AIDS testing, prenatal care; will make appointments.

Safe Sex Info: REDA Project—Really learn about safe sex!

Substance Abuse Help: Women's Alcoholism Center—Drug and alcohol rehab information.

Blood Pressure Check: provided by UCSF Nurses.

Eye Exams: Sign up to win a free eye exam and glasses.

MediCal Info: MediCal outreach representative on site.

EDUCATION/JOBS

College Info: City College—come meet the Dean of the Mission campus and find out about classes and financial aid.

Resume and Job Hunting Advice: Mission Hiring Hall and Jewish Vocational Services—a professional can help you with your resume and job search.

GAIN: Vocational training for AFDC moms.

PARENTING

Parental Stress: T.A.L.K. Line—Information on services for parents.

Child Care: Child Care Law Center—Information on how to find good, affordable child care in San Francisco.

Head Start: EOC Head Start—Register your pre-school children for this great program.

4K

STATE BAR OF CALIFORNIA

HOW DO I USE THE SMALL CLAIMS COURT?

GET THE LEGAL FACTS OF LIFE

State Bar of California
555 Franklin Street
San Francisco, CA
94102-4498

Recycled Paper

Place Stamp Here

How Do I Use the Small Claims Court?

1 What kinds of disputes can I take to small claims court?

2 What can I do if I am owed more than the small claims limit?

3 Is small claims court the best way to handle my claim?

4 How does the small claims court work?

5 How do I file my claim?

6 What if I have a claim against the person who is suing me?

7 What should I do before going to court?

8 What should I bring to court with me?

9 What happens if I do not show up for the hearing?

10 If I lose, can I take the case to a higher court?

11 What if the judge decides against me but I have a problem paying?

12 How do I collect my money?

1 What kinds of disputes can I take to small claims court?

You can use the small claims court if you h a dispute with a person, company or governmer agency involving $5,000 or less.

You might want to take a dispute to small court — which is called "making or filing a clair for example:

- Someone dents your fender and refuses to pa repairs.
- Your new sofa comes apart at the seams, and store will not fix it or give back your money.
- The dry cleaner ruins your favorite shirt and w pay you anything.
- The landlord will not return your security depc even though you left the apartment in good cor
- You loaned money to someone who will not p back.

2 What can I do if I am owed more than the small claims limit?

You may want to hire a lawyer and sue in higher court. Or, you may cut your claim to fit t $5,000 limit.

For example, if a person owes you $5,40 can give up $400 in order to bring your claim d the $5,000 limit. However, you cannot sue the twice — once for $5,000 and then for $400.

Also, keep in mind that you cannot file m two claims for more than $2,500 each in the sa year.

When you take a dispute to small claims you may be entitled to receive "costs" from th person. These are such charges as filing fees, costs of notifying the person you are suing anc ness fees. Ask the court to add these costs to "judgment," which is the amount of money th court says the other person owes you.

3 Should we settle out of court?

You must decide whether the small claims court is the best answer to your problem. You will have to spend some time getting ready for a court hearing. You also may have to take time off work to visit the small claims court clerk's office and to attend the hearing.

Even if you win, the person you sued may not have the money to pay you. Then, you will need to spend more time and money trying to collect. If you do not have time to collect the money yourself, you may hire a collection agency. The agency may charge a fee of up to 50 percent of the money it collects.

Instead of going to court, you can consider:

- **Dealing directly with the other party.** Both of you may end up saving time and money if you can agree on a way to settle the dispute. Let's say that you are the person being sued. If someone says you owe $300, you might say "I think you are wrong about that, but I would be willing to pay you $150 so that we can both forget it." If you do this, be sure to have a written agreement and keep a signed copy in a safe place. Also, check with the clerk of the small claims court to be sure that the lawsuit is dismissed.
- **Arbitration.** If your dispute involves a contract, check to see if the contract includes the right to arbitrate in case of a disagreement. This means you can submit the contract dispute to an independent, impartial panel that will hear both sides and recommend a solution. If you file a suit in small claims court, you may give up the right to arbitrate the dispute later.
- **Mediation.** This means that a "neutral third party" — a person who is not involved in the dispute — tries to help you and the other party come to an agreement. Mediation is voluntary, and mediators do not give their opinions. Instead, they help people exchange information and ideas and talk about ways to settle their differences. Check with the small claims court clerk to see if there is a mediation center in your area.

4 [illegible] does the small claims court [illegible]

In most instances, lawyers are not allowed in small claims court, so you must represent yourself. However, you can talk to a lawyer beforehand (see #7). This is true whether you are the "plaintiff" — the person who is suing — or the "defendant" — the person being sued.

Small claims courts are informal. They do not have complicated ways of doing things. No one is allowed to make objections. And there are no juries.

Cases move quickly. Usually, a hearing is scheduled within 40 days. However, if one of the people involved lives outside the county, it might take up to 70 days.

You do not have to be a United States citizen to use the small claims court. You do have to be at least 18 years old and mentally competent. If you are not, the court must appoint a "guardian" — parent, relative or adult friend — to sue for you.

When you file your claim, the court clerk generally will set the hearing date. In larger communities, small claims court is held some evenings or on Saturday once a month.

Also, many counties have a small claims advisor who can answer your questions and explain the process. An advisor also may be able to help you find a mediation service (see #3). Usually the information on contacting the small claims advisor is included on instructions available from the court.

5 [illegible]

Before you file a claim, you must demand payment from the other person when possible, and that person must refuse to pay or ignore your demand. It is a good idea to make the demand in writing and to keep a copy.

Most personal injury claims must be filed within one year. But claims dealing with property damage, written contracts and many other problems can be filed even after a year has passed. Also, time limits — and procedures — are different if you want to sue a federal agency. So, be sure to ask the small claims advisor for information.

Here are three basic steps in filing a claim:

Step 1: Fill out and sign a "Claim of Plaintiff" form. You will need this information:

■ **The right place.** You need to file your claim in the proper courthouse. Depending on the reason you are suing, this can be where the dispute took place, where the person you are suing lives, where the firm you are suing does business, where the contract you made was supposed to be fulfilled, where the contract was entered,or where the accident that led to your dispute took place. Check with the small claims advisor, who you can contact through your county small claims court, to be sure you file in the right place.

■ **The defendant's proper name.** This is very important. If you do not correctly state the name of the person or company in your claim, the case may be dismissed. Then, you may have to start over. An incorrect name also may cause problems when you try to collect money from the defendant.

If you sue individuals, you will need each person's full name and address. For a business, you will need the names of the company and the owners. When a corporation is involved, be sure to get its full name and address. You also need the name and address of an officer or some other person that legally can be notified of a lawsuit. You can get this information about corporations that do business in California from the Corporate Status Division, Secretary of State, 1230 J Street, Sacramento, California 95814.

If the case involves a car accident, it is very important to get the full name and address of the registered owner and the driver — if they are not the same person. You also can ask for the name of the car's legal owner.

■ **The facts of the dispute.** You must know exac how much money you are claiming, the reason wh you are claiming the money, and the date and plac that the dispute got started.

Step 2: Pay the filing fee. If you cannot afford fee or any other costs involved, you may not have pay. Ask the clerk for a "fee waiver form."

Step 3: Notify the defendant. You must arran have a copy of the Claim of Plaintiff "served" or d ered to each defendant you are suing. The law say that any person who is 18 or older and who is not involved in the case can deliver the notice.

There are four ways in which you can notify defendant. You can arrange to have someone from sheriff's, marshal's or constable's office serve the notice. Although it costs more, you can hire a "pro server" to make the delivery. The court clerk can the notice for you by certified mail for a small fee for each defendant. Or, a friend over 18 years old act as a process server for you.

If you win the case, you may be able to get the cost of serving the Claim of Plaintiff.

If you use a process server or a friend, be s the person completes and signs the form saying the notice was delivered to the defendant. This n is called "Proof of Service." The person also mus return the form to the small claims clerk's office. friend also must understand that the Claim of Pla must be served personally on the person being s or proper substituted service (see below); it cann left on a doorstep or stuffed into a mailbox.

Defendants must receive the Claim of Plair least 10 days before the hearing, if they live in th county where it will be held. If they live outside t county, they must receive it at least 15 days befo hearing. Otherwise, unless a defendant chooses show up and says "let's go ahead anyway," the must delay the hearing for at least 15 days.

In some cases, you may be able to use "su tuted service." This means that someone other the defendant can receive the notice that you ar and a copy mailed to the defendant. See your sr claims advisor to find out if you can, or should, use substituted service.

6 What if I have a claim against the person who is suing me?

First, you must demand that the person pay you the exact amount that you believe you are owed. If you do not receive the money, you may file a "Claim of Defendant" against the plaintiff. This is a paper that says how much the other person owes you and why.

You can get the form from the small claims clerk. Do this well before the hearing date because, in most cases, the person suing you must receive the form at least five days before the hearing.

You must serve the Claim of Defendant the same way that a Claim of Plaintiff is served (see #5).

7 [illegible]

Try not to be nervous. Keep in mind that the judge — or mediator, in some cases — is experienced in settling disputes and will try to come to a fair decision.

If you think you will have trouble remembering all the facts or talking to the judge, write down a list of the important points so you won't forget anything. Or, have someone write the list for you. Then, rehearse what you want to say in front of a friend, a family member or a mirror. If necessary, you can read your remarks to the judge. But do not plan to make a long statement.

You also can ask the small claims court advisor to help you prepare for the hearing. And although you cannot take a lawyer to court with you, you have every right to talk with one beforehand. If you want to talk to a lawyer and do not know one, you can ask a friend, a co-worker, your employer or a business person to recommend one.

Or, call your local State Bar-certified lawyer referral service. Look in the Yellow Pages of your telephone directory under "Attorney Referral Services," "Attorneys" or "Lawyers." The person who answers your call can make an appointment for you to see a lawyer. Usually, you will pay a small fee to talk with the lawyer for about half an hour. If you need to hire the lawyer for additional help, make sure you understand what you will be paying for, how much it will cost and when you will be expected to pay your bill. You can ask to have this information in writing.

What if you do not have enough money to pay for legal advice? You may belong to a "legal insurance" plan that covers the kind of services you need. Or, if your income is very low, you may qualify for free or low-cost legal help. Check the white pages of your telephone directory for a legal aid society in your county. You also can ask your county bar association if its lawyer referral service offers free legal advice for low income people or if it can direct you to a no-cost legal services organization.

For more information, write the State Bar for a free copy of its pamphlet, *How Can I Find and Hire the Right Lawyer?* Please be sure to enclose a stamped, self-addressed envelope with your request for a quick response.

8 [illegible] ould [illegible] bring to court with [illegible]

Be sure to bring the original copies of all the papers that you need to prove your case. For example bring any letter, contract, rental agreement, deed, canceled check, repair bill, I.O.U., written damage estimate, diagram, drawing or photograph that will help your case. You also should bring two photocopies of every original. You may be asked to give one copy to the person you are suing and one to the court. Depending on the reason you are going to court, you might even bring the shirt that a dry cleaner ruined or the blender that does not work.

If you have any witnesses, you must bring them court with you. The judge generally will not consider hat a witness has to say unless the person says it in urt. But, if your witnesses cannot appear in court, ng signed statements or "declarations" just in case e judge allows them. If possible, have the state- ents notarized.

If a witness refuses to attend, the court can issue "subpoena" — an official paper ordering the person come. The small claims clerk can tell you how to do s. If you subpoena a witness, you must be prepared pay that person a set fee each day plus a certain nount per mile to and from the court. Be sure to ask e judge at the hearing to add these costs to the judg- ent (see #2).

Make a brief statement of the facts, covering the portant points. Answer the judge's questions care- ily. Do not insult or argue with the other party, no atter how angry you get.

Sometimes the judge announces the decision at e end of the hearing. But often the case will be taken nder "submission," which gives the judge time to eview the law carefully. In this case, you will receive e judge's decision in writing in about two weeks.

What happens if I do not show up for the hearing?

If you are the defendant and cannot go to court at e time of the hearing, write the small claims clerk as oon as possible. Ask if you can get the date changed.

Otherwise, if you are properly notified about the earing and do not show up, the judge is likely to order "default judgment" against you. This means the ourt — after hearing evidence from the other side — as decided against you.

If you are the plaintiff and you do not show up, e judge may dismiss your case or decide in favor of e defendant.

In either case, to get a second chance to tell your side of the story, there must be a very good reason why you did not attend the hearing. If you think the judge will accept your reason, file a motion to "vacate the judgment." You must do this within 30 days of the date that the clerk mailed you the notice of the court's decision. The clerk will give you the forms to fill out. If you do not file this motion, you will not be allowed to appeal the decision to a higher court either.

10

Only defendants can "appeal" or ask a higher court to hear the case. So, if you are the plaintiff, you cannot appeal — unless the defendant files a "Claim of Defendant" (see #6) against you, and you lose this case.

If you believe that the judge has made a "clerical error," be sure to tell the small claims court clerk. For example, the amounts due you may have been added incorrectly.

You must file an appeal with the clerk in munici- pal or justice court within 30 days after the notice of the decision is mailed. You also must pay certain fees. The superior court then will hear your case all over again. In this court, both you and the plaintiff may have lawyers to represent you.

A word of caution: If you lose an appeal in a high- er court, you may be ordered to pay the judgment plus interest, costs involved and the plaintiff's attorney's fee up to $150. You may even have to pay up to $1,000 in attorney's fees if the judge decides your appeal had no real basis and was not brought in good faith. You could also be held responsible for the other parties transportation and lodging.

11 What if the judge decides against me but I have a problem paying?

You can ask the judge if you can make installment payments. Otherwise, the sheriff can take your wages or other property in order to pay the money you owe. You cannot be sent to jail, though, for failing to pay a debt.

12 [illegible] collecting [illegible] money?

The small claims court cannot collect your money for you, but the clerk or small claims advisor can tell you about some ways to do this yourself.

For example, you may be able to have the defendant's wages "garnished." This means that the person's employer gives you part of the defendant's wages each pay day until the debt is paid. To collect your money this way, you must find out where the person works; be sure to get the name of the company and its full address, including the county. Then, ask the small claims court clerk for a "Writ of Execution" and fill it out. When the court issues this writ, the sheriff or marshal will deliver it to the debtor's employer.

If you know where the defendant banks, the small claims clerk can issue a "Writ of Execution" that the sheriff or marshal takes to the bank. You need to know the name of the bank, the full branch address and the county. The bank will pay you what is owed, if there is enough money in the account.

A "Writ of Execution" also can be used to "attach" or take certain kinds of personal property, such as stocks, bonds and the contents of a safe deposit box. After this property is collected, it can be sold in order to pay the money that you are owed.

Not all personal property can be taken. The defendant can file a "Claim of Exemption" to protect the "necessities of life," possibly including a house, furniture, clothes and some wages.

The cost of a Writ of Execution — as well as the amount that the sheriff or marshal charges to deliver the writ — can be added to the amount that the defendant owes you. You also are entitled to interest during the time it takes to collect.

If you do not have the information you need to collect your money, you can make the defendant come to court and answer your questions about wages, the employer's location, bank account, personal property and real estate. Contact the small claims advisor for information about how to schedule this hearing.

Remember: The judgment is good for 10 years, and you can renew it if you still have not collected the amount you are owed. But, in many cases, the longer you wait, the harder it is to collect the money.

The purpose of this pamphlet is to provide general information on the law, which is subject to change. If you have a specific legal problem, you may want to consult a lawyer.

PRO BONO HOTLINE

I. PROJECT DESCRIPTION

Many legal aid societies are unable to meet the needs of their communities. To address the problem, the Young Lawyers Section of the Virginia Bar Association ("VBA") and Central Virginia Legal Aid Society, Inc. ("CVLA") co-sponsor the Pro Bono Hotline (the "Hotline") in Richmond, Virginia.

Each afternoon two VBA volunteer lawyers go to the offices of CVLA and call approximately 25 clients of CVLA who called the previous day with questions in the areas of consumer, domestic, employment or housing law. The volunteers are able to provide prompt advice to approximately 62.8% of such clients and such cases are closed. Other clients are given appointments. When the volunteer leaves the Hotline, no follow up is required, therefore, each volunteer has a maximum annual time commitment.

II. PROJECT PLANNING/DEVELOPMENT

A. Identification of Need

A 1990 study conducted by the Virginia Commonwealth University, Richmond, Virginia determined that 80% of the need for legal aid in civil cases is unmet in Virginia. Many of these individuals cannot pay for legal services and do not have access to transportation to meet with an attorney. To try to meet this need, CVLA began to operate a hotline using its staff attorneys. The increase in its case load was too great and CVLA abandoned the project. During the fall of 1992, CVLA asked the VBA for assistance in implementing a Hotline using volunteer attorneys.

A Young Lawyer Division ("YLD") interested in establishing a Hotline should contact its local Legal Aid. Together Legal Aid and YLD should determine whether Legal Aid is serving all of its potential clients. To determine the need, Legal Aid may want to run a trial Hotline using its staff attorneys. If Legal Aid and YLD determine that all potential clients are not served, they next should determine what discrete subject areas of the law a Hotline could serve.

B. Determination of Project Goals and Design

1. Decisions to Be Made

a. Options - Project Goals

The Hotline has the primary goal of providing prompt legal advice to CVLA clients who previously did not receive legal services. Telephone advice was viewed as the best way to provide prompt legal service. The format of having volunteers return phone calls was required because of potential conflicts.

b. Options - Project Design

The VBA and CVLA quickly determined that a Hotline manned by volunteers who return calls to clients was the best way to meet the need. Because CVLA had tested the format using its own attorneys, it knew that many cases could be handled promptly on the telephone. As stated above, returning telephone calls is required because of potential conflicts.

CVLA and the VBA determined that the Hotline should respond to calls in only limited subject areas. By limiting the subject matter, volunteers could receive full training in those areas. CVLA concluded that the volunteers could be most helpful in the areas of consumer, domestic, employment and housing law. A Hotline in different sized communities could vary the number of areas.

The size of the program was determined by estimating the number of inquiries that CVLA receives in the subject areas that could be handled by volunteer attorneys. Each volunteer is able to return approximately 10-15 calls in four hours.

2. Decision Making Process

Because the Hotline is a joint project between the VBA and CVLA, most of the decisions are made by deliberations between VBA and CVLA. CVLA approached the VBA to ask for the VBA's help in starting the Hotline. The continued excitement about the project resulted in the involvement of the Senior Section and Young Lawyers Section Executive Committee of the VBA. The Senior Section and the Executive Committee assisted in the recruitment of volunteers for the Hotline.

3. Considerations in Project Planning

a. Community Resources

The only community resources required are a strong Legal Aid society and a service-oriented bar community. A YLD interested in implementing a Hotline should contact the executive director of its local Legal Aid.

b. Personnel

To operate a Hotline with two volunteers four days a week, approximately 60 attorneys are needed. Each of the volunteers devote 50 hours per year to the Hotline in addition to the 12 hours of training. Without a responsible and devoted group of volunteers, the Hotline cannot succeed. A VBA committee of two chairpersons oversees the project.

CVLA devotes three people to the Hotline. A staff person prepares the conflict list each day and sends it to the next day's volunteers. A CVLA attorney is designated to oversee the Hotline each day. He or she answers questions the volunteers may have, reviews with volunteers the advice given and is responsible for any follow up action that is necessary. Finally, one attorney of CVLA manages the project for CVLA.

c. Revenue Availability/Fundraising

A Hotline that operates four days per week costs approximately $7,000 in its first year. Copy costs for the course materials make up approximately $4,000 of such costs. Recruiting, training and communicating with volunteers also is expensive. These costs include postage, fax charges, transportation costs for any out-of-town speakers during training and providing meals for volunteers and speakers during the training. Both CVLA and the VBA provide funding for the project out of their budgets. Both have applied for and received grants for the project from local and national sources, including an ABA Affiliate Outreach Project grant.

In addition, law firms have given in kind contributions of both time and resources. For example, the rate charged for copying of course materials was reduced substantially.

d. Equipment/Physical Needs

The daily operation of the Hotline requires two telephones and an office at Legal Aid and a telecopy machine at Legal Aid for sending the conflict reports.

The training of the volunteers requires a conference room large enough for most of the volunteers. In addition, the affiliates videotaped the sessions for use by volunteers who could not attend in person.

III. IMPLEMENTATION

A. Timetable

Below is an aggressive schedule for commencing a Hotline. The time between deciding to operate a Hotline and recruiting volunteers may need to be longer depending on circumstances.

Day 1: YLD Hotline co-chairs meeting with the executive director of Legal Aid to determine the need for a Hotline in the community.

Day 8: Optional: To determine whether a Hotline would serve an unmet need, Legal Aid begins operation of a Hotline using staff attorneys. Calls in designated areas are forwarded to an attorney who gives telephone advice to clients.

Day 45: Hotline co-chairs meet with Legal Aid to confirm that Hotline will meet the unmet need. Together they determine:

(i) number of days of operation;

(ii) number of volunteer attorneys needed each day;

(iii) total number of volunteers needed;

(iv) subject matter of calls answered by Hotline;

(v) tentative dates for training; and

(vi) tentative date to begin operation of the Hotline.

Day 60: YLD begins recruitment of volunteers - mass mailing and memorandum circulated within firms.

Day 61: Legal Aid finds speakers for training sessions.

Day 90: YLD begins targeted recruiting of volunteers - attorneys in senior section and YLD executive committee provide assistance.

Day 91: Legal Aid begins preparing course materials and Deskbook.

Day 105: 1st Day of Training - 2 to 3 hours on first subject. Circulate list of preferred days to volunteers.

Day 107: 2nd Day of Training - 2 to 3 hours on second subject. Circulate list of preferred days to volunteers.

Day 112: 3rd Day of Training - 2 to 3 hours on third subject. Circulate list of preferred days to volunteers.

Day 114: 4th Day of Training - 2 to 3 hours on fourth subject. Circulate list of preferred days to volunteers.

Day 115: YLD makes videotapes for training sessions available to volunteers.

Day 118: YLD circulates calendar for first four months of operation.

Day 119: Legal Aid prepares pamphlets to mail to clients.

Day 128: Commence operation of Hotline.

B. Recruiting and Training of Volunteers

The recruiting and training of volunteers is the most time consuming and expensive aspect of the Hotline. Our first recruiting effort was a mass mailing to all young attorneys in Richmond, Virginia of a letter and an article about the Hotline that had appeared in the VBA newsletter. The letter stressed the guaranteed limited time commitment and 12 hours of training that would qualify for CLE credit. At the same time, attorneys in each of the larger firms in Richmond circulated a memorandum to the associates in their firms. Approximately 50% of the Hotline's volunteers resulted from such mass mailing and memorandum.

Our second recruiting effort involved a targeted mailing. The co-chairs reviewed a list of all the VBA attorneys in Richmond and wrote a personalized letter to each attorney they knew. In addition, attorneys in the Senior Section and the Young Lawyer Section Executive Committee of the VBA contacted attorneys at their firms and encouraged their volunteering for the Hotline. The targeted efforts recruited the other volunteers.

Each volunteer committed to volunteer at the Hotline for one year. About 10% of the volunteers needed to leave the program during the year because of personal reasons. Because of the necessity to train volunteers, recruiting of volunteers occurs only annually. Therefore, more volunteers than initially needed should be recruited.

In the ninth month of the year, each volunteer was asked by telephone to commit to an additional year. Each volunteer was also asked how the Hotline could be improved and whether they would recommend volunteering at the Hotline to a colleague. In addition, a targeted mailing to all recent law school graduates was made.

CVLA was responsible for the training of the volunteers. The VBA assisted by making the arrangements for the training sessions. Volunteers received approximately three hours of training on each of the four areas of the law covered by the Hotline. CVLA prepared course materials on each of the topics. Volunteers use these materials for training and to assist them with answering questions at the Hotline. In addition, CVLA prepared a Deskbook that includes: (i) advice on handling certain types of calls; (ii) addresses and phone numbers of public agencies; and (iii) CVLA polices on accepting and excluding cases.

The best course materials and speakers provided specific advice on how to respond to typical questions. We have found that if a client asks complicated questions, it is best to make an appointment to speak to a CVLA attorney; therefore, the goal of the training should be to prepare the volunteers for answering typical questions asked by clients of Legal Aid.

The training materials prepared by a YLD could be used by different Hotlines throughout its state of operation. Each Legal Aid would need to prepare its own Deskbook.

We used our training sessions to explain the mechanics of operating the Hotline and to express our thanks for volunteering. The training sessions are the only time more than two volunteers are gathered together. Therefore, we do not recommend only using a videotape to train the volunteers. However, it could be effective to supplement a videotape of the substantive portion of the training with a live presentation.

A set of the course materials costs approximately $65 per volunteer. By focusing the materials on topics most often asked of volunteers, the length of the materials and cost could be decreased. Because our training occurred in the evening, we provided dinner to the volunteers at a cost of approximately $150 per training session. A YLD with a limited budget could request that the volunteers bring their own dinners, or schedule the training on a Saturday and have the volunteers bring their own lunch.

C. Publicity

The VBA wrote numerous articles in its newsletter about the Hotline. The articles followed the development of the Hotline from conception to successful operation. The articles were aimed toward encouraging attorneys to volunteer at the Hotline and proved helpful when recruiting volunteers.

D. Day-to-Day Operations

Every four months the volunteers receive a schedule of the days he or she will be volunteering. Three volunteers are listed for each day the Hotline operates. One of the volunteers is listed as an alternate. Each of the three volunteers must be from a different law firm; if one volunteer has a conflict with a client, the other volunteer is able to return the call.

If a volunteer is unable to operate the Hotline, he or she calls the alternate. If the alternate is unavailable, the primary volunteer is encouraged to find a substitute. If no substitute is found, the Hotline operates with one volunteer.

In the course of its normal telephone intake, CVLA screens calls for the Hotline. If a caller meets the financial eligibility requirements of CVLA and has a non-emergency question in the areas handled by the Hotline, the caller is told that an attorney will call him or her the next afternoon. However, if the client calls after 3:00 p.m. or on a Thursday, the caller is told that an attorney will call him or her in two days. The Hotline does not operate on Fridays.

At approximately 3:00 p.m. each afternoon, CVLA telecopies to the next day's volunteers and alternate the list of clients and potentially adverse parties. Before reporting to the Hotline, the volunteer will conduct a conflicts check using the telecopied list. In some cases, a volunteer has notified CVLA that it can never give advice in certain areas because of subject matter conflicts. The telecopy also serves as a reminder that the volunteer is scheduled for the next afternoon.

Two volunteers arrive at CVLA at approximately 1:30 each afternoon. Occasionally, only one volunteer is required, and CVLA will call one volunteer to tell him or her she is not needed. Each volunteer is given a form for each client he or she will be calling. The form indicates the client's name, the adverse party and case type. The volunteer keeps notes on the form and indicates the advice given. On a separate form, the volunteer maintains a list of clients he or she called and what further action is necessary, if any.

While making the calls, the volunteer refers to the course books and Desktop handbook. If the volunteer has questions, he or she may call the CVLA attorney that has been assigned to oversee the Hotline that day (the "CVLA Attorney") or other attorneys at CVLA.

The volunteer has several ways to assist a client. He or she may give advice only and recommend that the case be closed. Alternatively, the volunteer may give advice and tell the client that he or she will be sent a pamphlet prepared by CVLA for use by the Hotline. If the client's question is complicated or relates to written materials, the volunteer provides general advice and tells the client that an appointment will be required. Although the volunteer has not closed the case, the advice is helpful because the client will be told to bring certain materials to the appointment. In rare cases, the volunteer will identify a problem that needs immediate attention, such as a quickly approaching court date or eviction. The volunteer transfers such a client to the emergency unit of CVLA.

After making all his or her calls, the volunteer meets with the CVLA Attorney and they discuss the client's questions and the advice given. If, in the judgment of the CVLA Attorney, different or further advice is required, the volunteer immediately calls the client to give the additional advice. The CVLA Attorney is responsible for implementing any further action, such as sending the pamphlets or making appointments.

When the volunteer leaves the Hotline, he or she has no further responsibilities until the day he or she next is scheduled to volunteer.

The co-chair's responsibility in the day-to-day operation of the Hotline is coordinating the volunteers. If a volunteer is unable to attend his or her session, he or she notifies the co-chairs. The co-chairs ask the volunteer to call an alternate volunteer. If the volunteer gives enough advance warning, the co-chairs will revise the calendar to accommodate the volunteer.

Hennepin County Bar Association

Jane L. Schoenike
Executive Director

Minnesota Law Center #350 • 514 Nicollet Mall • Minneapolis, MN 55402-1021 • Phone 612-340-0022
Fax 612-340-9518

TEL-LAW (612) 332-2114

TEL-LAW is a collection of 75 recorded messages written by lawyers to provide general information on a variety of legal topics. TEL-LAW can be accessed from any touch-tone phone, 24 hours a day, seven days a week, at no cost to local callers. Messages are three to six minutes long and are presented in straightforward, easy-to-understand language. Established in 1980 by the Hennepin County Bar Association as a service to the public, TEL-LAW now handles approximately 1,000 calls a month.

Accessing the service is simple. Callers dialing the TEL-LAW number, (612) 332-2114, hear a brief introduction and are then directed to enter the three digit code number of the message they wish to hear. A directory of all recorded messages can be heard by pressing zero.

TEL-LAW messages are regularly updated and re-recorded to stay current with the changes in the law. New messages are added as the need arises. The HCBA is currently in the process of translating the TEL-LAW messages into Spanish.

TEL-LAW brochures explaining the service and providing a directly of all available messages are distributed free-of-charge to organizations who supply such information to the public.

TEL-LAW DIRECTORY

TEL-LAW is a free telephone library of recorded legal information available 24 hours a day by touchtone phone.

Legal Services	
Legal Help in the Twin Cities	101
Legal Help outside the Twin Cities	102
Legal Aid Society of Minneapolis	103
Legal Aid of Ramsey County	104
Legal Advice Clinics	105
Chrysalis, help for women	106
Lawyer Referral Services	107
LAMBDA Justice Center	108
If your attorney charges too much	111
If your attorney has acted unethically	112
Mediating disputes	113

Credit & Bankruptcy	
Can bankruptcy help me?	120
Filing for bankruptcy	121
Applying for credit and loans	122
Dealing with credit bureaus	124
Is your home protected from creditors?	127
Wage garnishment	128

Landlord & Tenant	
What the law says about eviction	130
Your day in eviction court	131
Possible eviction defenses	132
Your rights in a mobile home park	134
Renting residential property: Leases and termination	145
Rights and duties of landlords	146
Rights and duties of tenants	147
Security and damage deposits	148
Repairs to rental property	149

Criminal Law	
If you are arrested	150
Making bail	151
Charged with a crime and can't afford to hire a lawyer	152
Driving and alcohol/drug testing	154

Civil Law	
Small claims or conciliation court	160
If you are sued	161
Collecting on a judgment	163

Family Law	
Legal separation	170
Annulment of a marriage	171
Divorce: "Dissolution of marriage"	172
Determining child custody through mediation	173
Custody of the children in a dissolution of marriage	174
How property is divided in a dissolution of marriage	175
How debts are divided in a dissolution of marriage	176
How financial support for children is determined	178
How financial support for a spouse is established	179
If child support is not being paid	180
A "summary dissolution" of marriage	181
Domestic Abuse	182
Adoption	183

Consumer Law	
Illegal sales gimmicks	200
Door to door sales	201
Buying a used car	203
MN's used car warranty law	204
MN's new car lemon law	205
Arbitration of auto warranty disputes	206
Odometer roll-backs	207
MN's "cooling off" law: the right to cancel	208
Credit card charge backs	209

Wills, Estates and Elder Concerns	
Do you need a will?	210
Probating an estate	211
Estate planning	212
Trusts	213
Gifts to minors	214
Joint tenancy	215
What taxes have to be paid when someone dies?	216
Persons in the commitment process	217
Guardianship and conservatorship for people who are unable to handle their own affairs	218
Living wills	219
Durable power of attorney for health care decisions	220

Juvenile Law	
Parents' liability for damages caused by children	225
Rights of juveniles who are detained	226
Children in need of protection or services	227

Tax Law	
If you failed to file an income tax return last year	230
If you can't meet the tax filing deadline	231

Employment	
Injured at work	250
If you lose your job	251
If your employer has treated you unfairly	252
Sexual harassment	253

Home Ownership	
So you want to sell your home	270
Protecting yourself when you build your own home	277
Protecting yourself when you buy a home	278
Protecting yourself when you buy a townhouse or condominium	279

Other Topics	
Patents, Trademarks & Copyrights	294
Libel & Slander	295

332-2114

Consumer Information: Attorney General's Office 612-296-33

Lawyers Professional Responsibility Board (also Tel-Law #112)
If you think your attorney has acted improperly 612-296-39

Attorney-Client Fee Arbitration (also Tel-Law #111)
If you think your attorney has charged too much 612-340-00

OTHER LEGAL RESOURCES

Legal Rights Center	871-4886	Disability Law Center	332-14
Migrant Legal Services	291-2837	Crime Victim Centers	340-54
Chrysalis Center for Women	871-2603	Centro Legal	291-01
Rape & Sexual [illegible]	[illegible]	[illegible]	

ADDITIONAL RESOURCES

ADDITIONAL RESOURCES

Resources Provided by the ABA Center for Pro Bono, a Project of the ABA Consortium on Legal Services and the Public

Pro Bono Hotline (312) 988-5769

Directory of Private Bar Involvement Programs
Contact: Bridget Howard (312) 988-5789

Directory of ABA Pro Bono Projects
Contact: Bridget Howard (312) 988-5789

Info Packs (Pre-Packaged Materials on the Operation of Private Bar Involvement Programs) Contact: See Attached Order Form

ABA Annual Pro Bono Conference
(Co-sponsored with the ABA Standing Committee on Lawyers' Public Service Responsibility)
Contact: Dorothy Jackson (312) 988-5766

Peer Consulting Project
Contact: Bonnie Allen (312) 988-5773

Statewide Pro Bono Support
Contact: Bonnie Allen (312) 988-5773

Rural Pro Bono Consortium
Contact: Bonnie Allen (312) 988-5773

Resources Provided by Other ABA Entities

Standards For Programs Providing Civil Pro Bono Legal Services To Persons Of Limited Means
Contact: See Attached Order Form

Innovative Fundraising Ideas For Legal Services and ***More...Innovative Fundraising Ideas for Legal Services***
Contact: See Attached Order Form

Law Firm Pro Bono Project
Contact: Esther F. Lardent (202) 942-5319

Litigation Assistance Partnership Project (LAPP)
A project of the ABA Section of Litigation that matches participating private law firms with legal services organizations and other entities for litigation assistance on public interest cases.
Contact: Ann Barker (423) 482-2173

A Business Commitment (ABC)
A project of the ABA Section of Business Law that matches pro bono business and transactional lawyers with legal services organizations, community development corporations, charitable organizations and other similar entities.
Contact: Guy Lescault (202) 452-0620

Statewide Planning Assistance Network (SPAN)
A partnership of the ABA and National Legal Aid and Defenders Association, SPAN provides leadership and assistance to state planning groups, bar associations, legal services providers and funders in the development and implementation of new state delivery systems.
Contact: Guy Lescault (202) 452-0620

ABA CENTER FOR PRO BONO

Info Pack

The American Bar Association Center for Pro Bono offers the following materials to help bar associations and legal services programs develop and operate effective pro bono projects utilizing the private bar in the delivery of legal services to the poor.

Info Packs

If you are interested in receiving any of the Info Packs listed below, please check the appropriate box. If there are additional materials you are interested in that are not currently on our list, please call the Pro Bono Hotline at 312/988-5769 and we will locate materials and/or resource persons for you.

- ☐ Case Priorities
- ☐ Clinics
- ☐ Conflicts of Interest in the Pro Bono Context
- ☐ Conducting Training Programs for Volunteer Attorneys
- ☐ Corporate Counsel Pro Bono Efforts and Ideas
- ☐ Creative Use of Attorney Volunteers
- ☐ Encouraging Judicial Participation in Pro Bono
- ☐ Fundraising
- ☐ Government Attorney Pro Bono Participation
- ☐ Immigration
- ☐ Involving Non–Attorney Volunteers in Your Program
- ☐ Job Descriptions and the Role of Staff
- ☐ Program Operations/Policy and Procedure Manuals
- ☐ Public Relations—How To's
- ☐ Recognizing Volunteer Attorney Efforts
- ☐ Recruiting for a Volunteer Attorney Program
- ☐ Rural Delivery
- ☐ Self–Assessment
- ☐ Self–Help Program Materials and Ideas
- ☐ Senior Lawyer Pro Bono
- ☐ State Ethical Rules and Bar Association Pro Bono Resolutions
- ☐ Strategic/Long Range Planning
- ☐ The Law of Pro Bono: Mandatory, Assigned Counsel and other Legal Issues
- ☐ Working Effectively with Advisory Boards

SHIPPING AND HANDLING: 1 to 5 Info Packs .... Free
6 or more Info Packs .... $1 each ($10 for 10, etc.)

Pro Bono Manager's Handbook

In addition to the Info Packs, the Center produces the *Pro Bono Manager's Handbook.*

☐ Please send me _____ copies of the *Pro Bono Manager's Handbook* at $10.00 each.

All orders with a charge must be prepaid

Please send this form and a check (if applicable) made payable to the American Bar Association to:
Helena Feinberg, Center for Pro Bono, American Bar Association, 541 N. Fairbanks Court, Chicago, IL 60611.
If there is no payment required, orders may be sent by fax to 312/988-5032 or e-mailed to feinbergh@attmail.com.

SHIP ORDER TO: ______________________________
NAME/ORGANIZATION

____
ADDRESS No P.O. Box Numbers Please

____
CITY/ZIP/STATE

____
TELEPHONE FAX

April 1996

ABA

ABA House of Delegates Adopts Pro Bono Standards

The ABA Standing Committee on Lawyers' Public Service Responsibility is pleased to announce that on February 5, 1996, the ABA House of Delegates adopted, without dissent, the Standards for Programs Providing Civil Pro Bono Legal Services to Persons of Limited Means.

Designed to furnish guidance to newly established pro bono programs and to provide a basis for improving and evaluating existing programs, the Pro Bono Standards will serve as an invaluable resource in efforts to develop high quality, efficient and effective pro bono legal services delivery systems.

Copies of the Pro Bono Standards will be available for purchase in late March through the ABA Service Center. An order form is attached below for your convenience.

PLEASE SEND ME:

_________ Copies of the *Standards for Programs Providing Civil Pro Bono Legal Services to Persons of Limited Means* (PC 4690007) $12.00 per copy

_________ Subtotal

_________ Tax:
Maryland include 5%
Washington, DC include 5.75%
Illinois include 8.75%

_________ Handling Charges:
$3.95 for orders totalling $10-24.99
$4.95 for orders totalling $25-49.99
$5.95 for orders over $50

_________ Total amount enclosed

NAME

FIRM/ORG.

ADDRESS

CITY/STATE/ZIP

PHONE NUMBER

MAIL TO: American Bar Association
Publication Order
P.O. Box 10892
Chicago, IL 60610-0892

PHONE: 312/988-5522 **FAX:** 312/988-5568 EXCH 3/96

Please allow 1-2 weeks for delivery. Thank you for your order.

Publication Order Form

Title	Quantity	Total
More... Innovative Fundraising Ideas for Legal Services (4290023) $5.00 each for 1-10 copies $3.00 each for over 10 copies	________	________
Innovative Fundraising Ideas for Legal Services (4290021) $5.00 each for 1-10 copies $3.00 each for over 10 copies	________	________

Sales tax for orders placed from:
Maryland include 5% for sales tax
Washington, DC, include 5.75% for sales tax
Illinois include 8.75% for sales tax

Sales Tax: ________

Handling Charges
For orders totaling $3-9.99 include $2.00
For orders totaling $10-24.99 include $3.95
For orders totaling $25-49.99 include $4.95
For orders over $50 include $5.95

Handling Charge: ________

Total: ________

Mail check made payable to American Bar Association to: American Bar Association, Publication Orders, P.O. Box 10892, Chicago, IL 60610-0892. Or call 312/988-5522.

Name ____________________

Firm or Organization ____________________

Address ____________________

City ____________ State ____________ Zip ____________

INDEX OF ATTACHMENTS

INDEX OF ATTACHMENTS

3-F Materials from Training Seminars, Sponsored by the Virginia State Bar and the Bar Association of the City of Richmond and Central Virginia Legal Aid Society

3-G Nomination Brochure for ABA Pro Bono Publico Awards

3-H Brochure for San Diego Volunteer Lawyer Program "Justice For All" Awards Dinner

4-A People's Pro Bono Action Center, Inc. (Maryland) Program Description

4-B Texas Lawyers Care Program Description

4-C Excerpt from Idaho Volunteer Lawyers Program Policy Council Handbook

4-D Job Description for Coordinator of State Bar of New Mexico "Lawyers Care" Project

4-E Description of Philadelphia Volunteers for the Indigent Program

4-F Description of Legal Aid Society of the Orange County Bar Association, Inc. (Florida) Pro Bono Program

4-G Description of Pro Se Divorce Clinic ,"Put Something Back" Project (Dade County, Florida)

4-H Description of Debt Collection Advice Clinic, Volunteer Legal Services Project of Monroe County (New York)

4-I Article in June, 1996 ABA Center for Pro Bono *Exchange*: "Court-Based Pro Bono"

4-J Description of the "One-Stop" Women's Clinic, Volunteer Legal Services Program of the Bar Association of San Francisco

4-K The State Bar of California Brochure on *How Do I Use the Small Claims Court?*

4-L Project Description, the "Pro Bono Hotline," Co-Sponsored by the Young Lawyers Section of the Virginia Bar Association and Central Virginia Legal Aid Society, Inc.

4-M Description of the Hennepin County Bar Association (Minnesota) "Tel-Law" Project